REGULAR BAPTIST PRESS

The Doctrinal Basis of Our Curriculum

A more detailed statement with references is available upon request.

- The verbal, plenary inspiration of the Scriptures
- Only one true God
- The Trinity of the Godhead
- The Holy Spirit and His ministry
- The personality of Satan
- The Genesis account of creation
- Original sin and the fall of man
- The virgin birth of Christ
- Salvation through faith in the shed blood of Christ
- The bodily resurrection and priesthood of Christ
- Grace and the new birth
- Justification by faith
- Sanctification of the believer
- The security of the believer
- The church
- The ordinances of the local church: baptism by immersion and the Lord's Supper
- Biblical separation— ecclesiastical and personal
- Obedience to civil government
- The place of Israel
- The pretribulation rapture of the church
- The premillennial return of Christ
- The millennial reign of Christ
- Eternal glory in Heaven for the righteous
- Eternal torment in Hell for the wicked

Alex Bauman, Editor

Who I AM: God's Self-Revelation
Adult Bible Study Student Book
Vol. 64 • No. 1
© 2015 • Regular Baptist Press
www.regularbaptistpress.org • 1-800-727-4440
Printed in U.S.A.

RBP0138 • ISBN: 978-1-62940-116-4

Contents

Preface

Who is God?

Both Moses and Israel had a lot to learn about God. He first introduced Himself to Moses as the I AM. That name became more and more meaningful over the course of many years and many blessings and trials. God revealed Himself as He directed Moses to lead Israel from slavery in Egypt, through the Red Sea, to Mount Sinai, into the wilderness, and finally to the doorstep of the Promised Land. God had crucial lessons for Israel to learn about His character and ways.

You have the privilege of coming alongside Moses and God's people to learn about the I AM. The lessons in this study will help you understand God as the Sovereign, Transcendent Helper, Promise Keeper, Redeemer, Leader, Provider, Instructor, Glorious God, Atoner, Gracious Giver, Powerful Proclaimer, Loving Lord, and Solid Rock. You will be challenged with a much deeper understanding of God. Pray you will grasp the lessons God so wisely wove through the narratives of His faithful leading of His people.

I AM
Sovereign

▶ **Scripture Focus**

Gen. 12:1–3; 49:8–12; Exod. 1; 2:1–22; Gal. 3:8, 13–16

Theme

God sovereignly executes His plan despite both human attempts to deny it and human blunders that threaten to derail it.

Memory Verse

"And the scripture, foreseeing that God would justify the heathen through faith, preached before the gospel unto Abraham, saying, In thee shall all nations be blessed" (Galatians 3:8).

GETTING STARTED

There are times as history unfolds that we have to scratch our heads and wonder where God is in all that is going on. We may even ask that same question as we face difficult circumstances in our own lives.

1. When have you questioned where God was as you surveyed what was going on in the world?

2. When, if ever, have you questioned whether God was sovereign in your life?

This study will show that God sovereignly executes His plan despite both human attempts to deny it, and human blunders that threaten to derail it.

God Declared His Plan

Israel's history began with God's call of Abraham. God called him to leave his homeland for a land He would show him. He promised Abraham that he would become a great nation and that his descendants would live in a specific land. Out of that great nation would come a blessing to all the nations of the earth (Gen. 12:1–3).

Genesis 12—50 record the history of Abraham and his descendants. God passed the Abrahamic covenant down to Abraham's descendants. Abraham's son Isaac had a son named Jacob. Jacob, later called Israel, had twelve sons by his wives Rachel and Leah and by his wives' two maidservants (35:22–26). Jacob loved Rachel more than Leah and consequently favored her older son, Joseph (37:3). Joseph was the second youngest among his twelve brothers. The ten older brothers hated Joseph because of Jacob's favoritism and because of Joseph's dreams of greatness (37:1–11). They seized on the opportunity to get rid of him by selling him into Egypt as a slave (37:12–36). In Egypt, Joseph rose to second in command when God allowed him to interpret Pharaoh's dream about seven years of bumper crops followed by seven years of severe famine (41).

Jacob and his family eventually moved to Egypt to escape the famine (46). Instead of seeking vengeance, Joseph proclaimed to his brothers, *Now therefore be not grieved, nor angry with yourselves, that ye sold me hither: for God did send me before you to preserve life* (45:5). Eventually all of Joseph's family, including his brothers and their families and his father, came to live in prominence in Egypt (47:1–12).

Jacob's Blessing of Judah

Jacob lived in Egypt until his death. Before he died, he blessed each of his sons (49:1–28). The blessing he gave to Judah, his fourth oldest son, is of particular importance. It helps us understand what God meant when He promised that Abraham's seed would be a blessing to all nations (12:3).

3. Read Genesis 49:8, 10. What does this blessing reveal about a
    future descendant of Judah?

Judah was to rule his brothers in some way. That did not happen in
Judah's lifetime. So the statement must refer to a yet-future fulfillment.

The blessing in verse 10 develops the profile of a victorious warrior
king. *Sceptre* refers to the wand of kingship that extends to between
the king's *feet*. *Shiloh* is a reference to the Messiah. The word *Shiloh* can
mean *to whom it belongs*, indicating that the scepter belongs to Christ.
The scepter, then, will remain with Judah until Christ comes to establish
His rule over Israel and the *people*, a plural noun that refers to multiple
people groups or nations. Christ's rule will be established on earth during
His future millennial Kingdom. The concept of Christ ruling nations is
an important theme in the Bible (Ps. 2:8; Dan. 7:13, 14; Rev. 5:5, 9). And it
partially reveals how the *seed* (Gal. 3:16) of Abraham will be a blessing to
all peoples (Gen. 12:3).

4. Read Galatians 3:8, 13–16. What is the primary way in which
    Christ is a blessing to the nations?

Genesis 49:11 and 12 describe Christ's future rule as a time of great
prosperity. Grapevines will be strong enough to tie donkeys to without
worry of the donkey breaking free. And juice from the grapes of those
vines will be so plentiful that people could use it to wash their clothes.

5. Assume you don't know the rest of the story of Jacob's descen-
    dants. Based on the Genesis 49 blessing, what would you expect
    to happen next in the narrative surrounding this large family?

All seemed well when the book of Genesis closed. God's people were
living in peace and in favor with Pharaoh in Egypt. God's plan seemed to

be perfectly acceptable as Abraham's descendants grew into a nation. But Exodus begins with a turnabout; life was no longer easy.

6. Read Genesis 15:13, 14. Why should the Israelites have known that life was not going to continue to be easy for them as a nation?

Jacob moved to Egypt with seventy people. By the time Exodus opens, his descendants had grown exceedingly; the land of Egypt was filled with Israelites (Exod. 1:1–7). God had been faithful to His promise to make of Abraham a great nation. Because the nation had grown, one might expect Israel to peacefully move out of Egypt and on to the Promised Land to claim what was theirs. But God had a much different plan in mind. He had much more to accomplish than simply getting His people to the Promised Land.

God Thwarted Pharaoh's Plans

A pharaoh arose who knew nothing of Joseph's contribution to Egypt (1:8). To him the exploding nation of Israel was a power threat (1:9, 10). He was concerned that the Hebrews might rebel if Egypt were attacked. Yet he needed the Hebrews to provide labor for his ambitious projects. So he came up with a plan for lowering the risk of a Hebrew rebellion.

7. Read Exodus 1:8–11. What was Pharaoh's plan A for lowering the risk of a Hebrew rebellion?

Pharaoh's ultimate goal was to prevent Israel from leaving the land. Eventually that goal would be shared by another pharaoh nearly a century later when Moses arrived back in Egypt as Israel's deliverer (cf. 5:1, 2). The first fourteen chapters of Exodus build to a climax as both God and the pharaohs seek to carry out their plans for Israel.

The pharaoh in charge when the book of Exodus opens liked having the Hebrews as slaves. Astutely he had them build him two cities that housed supplies and most likely armaments that would help Egypt defeat any invading army. Notice that Pharaoh accounted for *human* enemies that might help the Hebrews but gave no thought about the Hebrews' God being a source of help. That the Hebrews were slaves in his land probably contributed to his low estimation of the Hebrews' God.

8. How do you think the Israelites felt about building cities that would solidify their state as slaves in Egypt?

9. Read Exodus 1:12. What became of Pharaoh's efforts to slow down Israel's growth as a nation?

The more Israel grew as a nation, the more worried Egypt became. The Egyptians began to become anxious about Israel's presence in their land.

Pharaoh responded to Israel's increase in strength and number by making the people work even harder. He made Israel work with *rigour*, meaning that the Egyptians treated the Hebrews harshly and drove them to work beyond reason (1:13, 14). Pharaoh's plan was to wear them out so that their desire to survive distracted them from the normal life of marrying and having children. Apparently Pharaoh's plan B didn't work. The Israelites continued to grow.

There is a sense in which the harder Pharaoh made the men of Israel work, the more they relished having a family to love and support them during the hours they were not being oppressed. Pharaoh's plan was in essence counterintuitive. Of course God's hand was also behind the scenes thwarting Pharaoh's plan B to keep the Israelites from growing as a nation.

10. When has a difficult circumstance helped you appreciate and grow closer to your family?

Still not seeing the results he wanted, Pharaoh tried plan C to deal with the population explosion at its source. He commanded the midwives to kill the Hebrew male babies as soon as they were born. Pharaoh wanted to destroy the future ranks of Hebrew soldiers. Perhaps he thought that at some point in the future he would let some Hebrew boys live to replenish his slaves that aged and were no longer able to work. For an ongoing policy of killing Hebrew boys would have eventually devastated Egypt's workforce.

11. Read Exodus 1:15–17. What kept the midwives from killing the Hebrew children?

Pharaoh soon realized that his plan C was not working. He called the midwives and asked them why they weren't obeying him. The midwives made up the excuse that the Hebrew women gave birth so quickly that they weren't even present to kill the baby boys. The midwives lied to Pharaoh and hid their reverence for God. Though God never condoned their lie, He did bless them because of their respect for Him in the matter of sparing the Hebrew boys.

Pharaoh became increasingly frustrated and desperate. So he enlisted all of the Egyptians to help him carry out his most cruel plan. He empowered every Egyptian to act as an executioner on his behalf. When the Egyptians saw a Hebrew baby boy, they were to execute the boy by throwing him into the Nile to drown.

12. Read Exodus 1:22. Describe what life would have been like for Hebrew families with Pharaoh's executioners lurking all around?

Chapter 1 ends with these awful circumstances in place. They became the new normal. It appears that Pharaoh had finally come up with a plan to keep Israel in Egypt. And we can safely assume that many of the Hebrews' boys were indeed drowned in the Nile.

13. What questions might you have been tempted to ask God if you had
been living as a Hebrew slave in Egypt at that point in history?

What God did next to continue to carry out His plan for His people
shows just how powerless Pharaoh was to keep God's people in Egypt.

God's Protective, Providential Hand

Perhaps Pharaoh thought that a death sentence for all Hebrew baby
boys would deter the Hebrews from having any children at all. But that
was not the case. A couple from the tribe of Levi married and had children. The couple is later identified as Amram and Jochebed. Their firstborn boy was Aaron (see 6:20). Their second boy was later named Moses.
Fearing Pharaoh's executioners, Moses' parents hid him for three months
until it became impossible to do so safely (2:1, 2).

14. Was keeping Moses safe for the first three months of his life up to
just Amram and Jochebed? Explain.

Jochebed made a watertight ark of bulrushes, put Moses in it, and
nestled it in the reeds by the bank of the Nile. Moses' sister Miriam stood
afar off to see what would become of her brother (2:3, 4).

One could argue that Jochebed was acting out of disbelief by taking
Moses out of hiding. But she was doing what God wanted. Her plan,
whether or not she realized it, was exactly what God wanted.

15. Read Exodus 2:5–9. What is your reaction when you read that God
used Pharaoh's daughter to protect Moses?

Pharaoh's efforts to keep the Israelites in Egypt were all part of
God's plan. God used the circumstances to allow Moses to safely return
home. There he most certainly received instructions about God and the

importance of his national identity as a Hebrew. The word used for *grew* indicates Moses was at least well into boyhood when he left to live with Pharaoh's daughter. Later he identified himself as a Hebrew rather than an Egyptian, even after spending most of his life in Pharaoh's house (cf. Acts 7:23–25). That national connection would be crucial for his leadership of Israel decades later.

What Moses did while he was in Pharaoh's household and under the care of Pharaoh's daughter is not well documented. But there are some clues and some conclusions we could draw.

16. Read Acts 7:21, 22. What did Moses learn while he was in Pharaoh's house?

Moses received leadership training while in Egypt. Later on he would balk at God's call to lead the Israelites out of Egypt, claiming he could not speak eloquently (Exod. 4:10). One could conclude that the leadership training he received in Egypt did him no good. But imagine how ill prepared he would have felt without his time in the Egyptian schools. Moses was *mighty in words*, meaning he commanded the language well and knew what to say on just about any subject. Being *mighty in . . . deeds* meant he had a good grasp of business and perhaps even war.

When Moses was forty, he went to visit his people and noticed an Egyptian beating a Hebrew (Exod. 2:11). Moses made sure no one was looking and then killed the Egyptian, burying his body in the sand (2:12). When Moses went out a second day to see the burdens of his people, he intervened in a dispute between two Hebrews. They questioned whether he would kill one of them as he had killed the Egyptian (2:13, 14). Moses realized that his murder of the Egyptian must have been made known. Moses fled Egypt as the report came to Pharaoh (2:15). Pharaoh was probably not as concerned about the murder as he was about Moses siding with the Hebrew slaves.

17. On the surface, what did Moses' blunder in killing the Egyptian seem to do to his opportunity to lead the Hebrews out of Egypt?

Moses ended up in Midian on the eastern shore of the Gulf of Aqaba. There he sat down by a well (2:15). Before long Moses was again intervening to stop an injustice. This time is was on the behalf of seven daughters of a Midianite priest named Reuel. Moses kept shepherds from chasing the daughters from the well (2:15–17). As a result, Reuel gave Moses his daughter Zipporah as his wife (2:18–22).

Moses remained in Midian for forty years (Acts 7:30). His life as a shepherd was far different than his life in Egypt.

18. What lessons would Moses learn from caring for sheep in the wilderness?

God providentially directed Moses' life to prepare Moses to lead the Hebrew slaves out of Egypt. God had already proved that He sovereignly executes His plan despite both human attempts to deny it and human blunders that threaten to derail it. Next He would introduce Himself to Moses as I AM, the transcendent helper.

MAKING IT PERSONAL

19. What obstacles to God's will for your life have you considered too big to overcome?

20. How should God's introduction of Himself as the Sovereign affect how you view those obstacles? Consider what God was able to do despite Pharaoh's attempts to deny His will.

21. Have you concluded that God could not use you because you've committed a blunder that seemed to derail His will for you?

22. Deal with those blunders, confessing any outstanding sins and renewing your relationship with God. Pray that God would use you to accomplish His will for your life.

I AM Transcendent Helper

▶ **Scripture Focus**

Exod. 2:23—4:17

Theme

God is both transcendently above us and eternally with us.

> ### Memory Verse
> *"And God said unto Moses, I AM THAT I AM: and he said,*
> *Thus shalt thou say unto the children of Israel,*
> *I AM hath sent me unto you" (Exodus 3:14).*

GETTING STARTED

A typical job interview ends with the interviewer asking the applicant if he has any questions about the position. A thoughtful applicant will most likely have some questions. But an applicant who starts grilling the interviewer with personal questions about his abilities and trustworthiness would most likely be shown the door.

1. What questions would you feel safe asking in a job interview?

2. What questions would you like to ask but wouldn't because you would be too afraid of the consequences?

God called Moses to a specific job. But it was Moses who seemed to be conducting the interview. He questioned both his own qualifications to do the job and God's fitness to be his boss. This study will examine Moses' questions for God as well as God's important self-revelation.

God Continued His Plan for Israel

Forty years had passed since Moses' departure from Egypt. God was ready to continue His plan for His people. When the account resumes, we learn that the king of Egypt who had chased Moses out of Egypt had died. A new pharaoh was in place, but the conditions in Egypt had not improved.

Israel groaned because the Egyptians worked them hard. Remember that the hard labor was meant to keep the Israelites from multiplying and from being strong enough to rebel. So, as they grew in number, their labor got harder. And the building projects they worked so hard to complete were making Egypt stronger and less vulnerable to being overthrown. From the Hebrews' perspective, their situation was becoming more and more desperate.

3. Read Exodus 2:23. Why is it significant that Israel's cry *came up unto* God? What does that phrase communicate about God?

The *aboveness* of God is an important theme in His continuation of His plan for Israel. We call this God's *transcendence*. He is inapproachably far above humanity. No one could possibly reach either His level of character or His ability. But God, though transcendent, still heard Israel's cry. That is a profound truth and one ripe with hope not just for Israel but for all humanity.

Though the Hebrew slaves in Egypt didn't yet know it, God had *heard* their groaning, *remembered* that He had made a covenant with them (2:24), *looked upon* them, and *had respect unto them* (2:25). God has been and always will be faithful to His promises to Israel. And His covenant with them is not an albatross around His neck. For God to *look upon*

His people was to *consider* their situation. They were important to Him. Though transcendent, He gave His attention to the slave nation in Egypt. And having *respect unto them* meant being *concerned* about them. He had a genuine desire to care for His people. He acted on their behalf out of covenantal love, rather than simply covenantal duty.

4. Read Jeremiah 31:3. How does God describe His love for Israel?

God Continued His Preparation of Moses

To rescue Israel, God needed to finish preparing Moses for the task. So He turned His attention to Moses, a shepherd who seemed to have become insignificant and even forgotten.

Moses led Jethro's flock to the west of Midian and came to what later became known as the *mountain of God* called *Horeb* (Exod. 3:1). Later Moses would end up at the same mountain as the shepherd of God's people (cf. 3:12; 19:1, 2).

The Angel of the Lord appeared to Moses in a burning bush that was not consumed by the fire. Moses turned aside to see this miracle. God then called to him (3:2–4). *Here am I*, Moses responded.

5. Read Exodus 2:23; 3:4. What is the connection between Israel's cry and God's call?

Later in the passage God said He had *come down* to rescue His people (3:8), a result of Israel's cries coming up to Him (2:23; 3:9).

God warned Moses not to draw near the bush (3:5). He instructed Moses to take off his shoes, for the ground was holy. This was a physical illustration of the transcendence of God. He had come down, but He was not on man's level. His holiness separated Him from man. God then introduced Himself as *the God of thy father, the God of Abraham, the God of Isaac, and the God of Jacob* (3:6). In response Moses hid his face, fearing to look on the manifestation of God before him.

6. Read Exodus 3:6. What did God's presence help Moses to understand about both himself and God?

Hiding his face was the appropriate response for Moses in the presence of God. He understood God's transcendence and sensed his own unworthiness to be in God's presence. He was more than willing to honor God's command to stay back from the burning bush.

God explained that He had come down because Israel's cries had come up to Him. Again, He communicated that He heard the people and knew their sorrows. His plan was to deliver His people and take them to *a land flowing with milk and honey* (3:7–9). The dichotomy of both God's transcendence and His eminence continued as God commissioned, instructed, and answered Moses.

God Commissioned Moses

God, having given His initial introduction and His reason for appearing, revealed Moses' involvement in His plan.

7. Read Exodus 3:10, 11. Can you identify with Moses' reaction? Explain.

Remember that Moses had left Egypt on the run. The pharaoh at that time wanted to kill him, and the Israelites had rejected his leadership, voicing their suspicion of his character (2:14). Those scenes must have come flooding back to Moses' mind. It is no wonder he resisted God's plan to send him to Pharaoh.

8. Read Exodus 3:12. What should have given Moses confidence as he returned to Egypt?

Don't miss the contrast between God demanding Moses not come near Him (3:5) and God's assurance that He would go *with* Moses to Pharaoh (3:12). God wanted Moses to understand both His transcendence and His eminence as He commissioned Moses. Moses would learn more about what it meant for God to be with him as God revealed to him more about His transcendent nature.

Moses wanted to know more about God. If God was going to go *with* him, what could he count on God to do *for* him? Moses didn't come right out and ask God what He was like. Instead he suggested that God's people in Egypt would like to know what God is like (3:13). Most likely the people *would* ask Moses about God's identity. Moses would need to know how to identify God. But perhaps Moses was also hiding his lack of confidence in God by removing the question from his lips and putting it on the Israelites' lips. His question was perhaps more to strengthen his confidence in God than it was to have answers for the Israelites. Moses' whole interaction with God is fraught with his personal doubt and fears.

God went along with Moses and answered his question in the context of the people of Israel (3:14). God told Moses that His name is *I AM THAT I AM*. That name means little to us, but in the Hebrew it was clear to Moses. The name *I AM* means God is self-sustaining. He is dependent on no one. He never had a beginning and will never have an end. He is outside time and space and infinitely big and powerful. In other words, He is transcendent. God is indescribably above all humanity.

9. Read Exodus 3:14. What would have been for Moses some of the implications of God's transcendence?

10. Read Exodus 3:15. What did God reveal about the longevity of His name?

God is still the *I AM* today. He is still far above us, yet He promises to be with us every moment of every day. What a privilege to personally know our transcendent God.

God Instructed Moses

God went right from His introduction of Himself as the I AM to His instructions for Moses, not pausing to give Moses an opportunity to question God's call on his life. Moses was to gather the elders of Israel and tell them that God had appeared to him (3:16). Again God called Himself the *God of your fathers* and specifically *of Abraham, of Isaac, and of Jacob*. It was important for the Hebrews to understand that Moses had talked with the same God Who had made a covenant with Abraham.

Moses was to communicate to the elders that God had visited His people and had seen what they were experiencing. Next Moses was to assure the elders that God would bring Israel out to the land flowing with milk and honey (3:17). The *withness* of God is emphasized in His message to His people. They needed to hear He had already been in their presence and would be with them to lead them to the Promised Land.

11. Read Exodus 3:18a. Why would Moses have had reason to doubt that the elders of Israel would heed his voice when he told them God's plan?

God put special emphasis on Moses' *voice* (3:18). Israel would heed his voice because God was with him. But even with God's special emphasis, Moses would later question whether the people would indeed listen to his *voice* (cf. 4:1).

God's initial message to Pharaoh was to be brief and limited. Moses was to tell Pharaoh to let God's people go three days' journey into the wilderness so they could worship God (3:18). This would mean that his building projects would remain idle for about a week. Pharaoh would not agree to let the Hebrews take a week's vacation to go into the wilderness to worship.

12. Read Exodus 3:19. What did God say would not compel Pharaoh to let Israel go?

The *mighty hand* is a reference to God's hand (3:19). Soon God would come down on Egypt with tremendous power and might. After the blows from God's hand, Pharaoh would give in and say he would let God's people go. But in each case Pharaoh would eventually respond by hardening his heart and refusing to let God's people go.

God's blows on Egypt would eventually move Pharaoh enough to let God's people get out of town (3:20). The people of Egypt would be so anxious to see Israel leave that they would give them gold, silver, and clothing (3:21, 22).

13. Why should Moses have had complete confidence in God at that point in his conversation with God?

God Answered Moses

Moses had not yet come to the point of completely trusting God as the I AM. He questioned God again. Remember, God was promising Moses that the people of Israel would listen to Moses' *voice* (3:18). But Moses wanted to play the *what if* game with God. He still thought God's people might not believe that God had actually appeared to him (4:1). The risk of rejection by God's people nagged him. He felt compelled to raise the what-if scenarios as if God had not thought through His plan or was powerless to bring about its outcome.

God patiently provided Moses with signs which would show that God had indeed appeared to him. First, God told Moses to throw his staff on the ground (4:2, 3). When he did, it became a snake. Moses, afraid of getting bit, ran from the snake (4:3). His reaction is normal. Everyone in their right mind recognizes the threat of a snake. But once Moses had a chance to consider what had just happened, he became emboldened, grabbing the snake by the tail as God instructed. Such an action almost always results in a snakebite. Instead, God turned the snake back into Moses' staff (4:4).

14. Read Exodus 4:3–5. How would you describe Moses' faith in God's power at this point in the narrative?

God added two more signs to demonstrate His power. First He made Moses' hand diseased and then healed it (4:6, 7). This sign would be a warning that God has power to inflict harm on the human body.

Next, Moses was to scoop water from the Nile as part of the third sign (4:9). The water would turn to blood as he poured it out. This sign sent a powerful message that was most likely not lost on both God's people and the Egyptians. The Nile was where Egyptians had murdered countless Hebrew boys as part of their plan to keep the Hebrews in Egypt. The blood from those Hebrew baby boys was, therefore, at one point in the Nile. God was well aware of that atrocity. The turning of the water to blood communicated His power over life, which was clearly seen in the death of the Egyptians' firstborn sons during the last plague (11:4–6).

God demonstrated His *aboveness* to Moses. He showed He is the transcendent One Who has unlimited power and knowledge and is therefore able to do whatever He desires.

Once God demonstrated by deed that He was worthy of Moses' trust, Moses became more direct in addressing his problem with God's plan. He flat out said he didn't think *he* had what it took to talk convincingly to God's people and to talk eloquently with Pharaoh.

15. Read Exodus 4:10, 11. Why was Moses' excuse an affront to God?

God told Moses not to worry about what to say or how to say it. He had made Moses' mouth exactly as He wanted it. He would be with Moses' mouth and *teach* him what he should say (4:12). God was again focusing on His presence *with* Moses.

16. What advantage might those with weaknesses or deficiencies have as they seek to serve God?

Moses, unconvinced of the sufficiency of God's presence, asked God to send someone else to Pharaoh (4:13). Moses didn't understand that God's call didn't have an escape clause. God was going to use Moses no matter what Moses decided. Moses would simply miss out on seeing the full extent of God's work. Moses would still lead, but Aaron's capable voice would be the main line of communication between God and His people. God would speak to Moses, who would pass on to Aaron the message to communicate to the people (4:14–17).

God is far above us. He is the I AM, needing no one to make Him complete, and remaining that way for all eternity. It is both God's power and His holiness that make Him far above us. We should never treat Him as trivial or as just another person.

17. Do you consider God's transcendence as you relate to Him? Explain.

18. How should you respond to God's transcendence?

God also assured Moses that He was *with* him. He *came down* to be *with* Moses and His people. God is not only with you, but He is also *in* you in the Person of the Holy Spirit.

19. How should you respond to God's presence with you?

I AM
Promise Keeper

▶ Scripture Focus

Exod. 4:18—7:13

Theme

God is trustworthy because He is promise-keeping Yahweh.

> ### Memory Verse
>
> *"Wherefore say unto the children of Israel, I am the LORD, and I will bring you out from under the burdens of the Egyptians, and I will rid you out of their bondage, and I will redeem you with a stretched out arm, and with great judgments"* (Exodus 6:6).

GETTING STARTED

We don't know all there is to know about one another. We all have sides of ourselves that no one else would ever guess. Perhaps you are a neatnik, keeping all your clothes neatly in your dresser drawers. Or maybe you are creative and you enjoy home decorating.

1. What side of you do most people not know about?

2. If you told them about that side of you, do you think they would believe you?

The more we learn about a person, the better we can relate to him and the closer we feel to him. God continued to reveal Himself to His people and to Moses. The passage this study includes God's revelation of Himself as Yahweh, the Promise Keeper.

God's Stated His Commitment to Israel

Perhaps out of courtesy, Moses returned from Sinai to Midian to ask Jethro for his permission to leave for Egypt (Exod. 4:18). Moses wanted to see how his brethren were doing. Jethro told Moses to *go in peace.*

God then came to Moses and directed him to return to Egypt. God's reference to the dead who had sought Moses' life (4:19) reminded Moses that he had tried to take the deliverance of God's people into his own hands. That turned out to be a major blunder. He ended up fleeing Egypt for his life. But here Moses was returning to Egypt according to God's plan and God's timing.

Moses saddled a donkey, put his family on it, and headed with them toward Egypt. His staff, once ordinary, became the *rod of God* in his hand (4:20). The rod was evidence of God's presence with Moses. Moses' family would become the center of a crisis as they journeyed, but first God had a message for Moses to help put the coming crisis into focus.

God gave Moses a personalized message to give to Pharaoh. God told Moses to refer to Israel as *my son, even my firstborn* (4:22). The sense of the word *firstborn* is *first in rank.* No people group on earth was more important to God at that time, and Pharaoh was holding them captive.

3. Read Exodus 4:23. Describe the seriousness of God's relationship with Israel.

4. How does considering Israel as God's *son* help you understand the commitment God had toward Israel?

God told Moses to tell Pharaoh to let His people go so they might *serve* Him (4:23). God essentially pitted Himself against Pharaoh, the one the Israelites served at that point. This theme of *God versus Pharaoh* is repeated throughout the account of the Exodus. It escalates to *God versus Pharaoh's gods* when God brings the plagues upon Egypt. It culminates when God takes the life of Pharaoh's son just as He said He would.

God Demanded Commitment from Moses

Following the statement of God's commitment to Israel is a shocking, seemingly out-of-place account of God confronting Moses. God seemed anything but committed to Israel when He threatened Moses, His chosen deliverer of Israel.

5. Read Exodus 4:24. What are your thoughts when you read this verse in the context of God's commitment to Israel?

God's anger with Moses must have been related to the rite of circumcision. While God detained Moses, his wife, Zipporah, circumcised Moses' son and cast the foreskin at Moses' feet. Zipporah accused Moses of being a *bloody husband* to her (4:25). Apparently Zipporah didn't think much of the rite of circumcision. She probably conducted the act out of fear for Moses' life. God forced her hand to ensure Moses' family performed the rite of the covenant. God let Moses go once the circumcision was complete (4:26).

6. Read Genesis 17:10–14. What was supposed to be the consequence of not performing the rite of circumcision?

This account reveals God demanded that Moses be committed to Him. God wanted Moses to honor Him and take the rite of circumcision seriously. He expected circumcision to be an outward sign of a heart for Him (cf. Deut. 30:4–6; Rom. 2:28, 29). How could Moses lead God's covenant people if he didn't practice the rite of circumcision with his own boys?

God prompted Aaron to meet Moses at Sinai (4:27). There Moses let Aaron know all that God had done and commanded (4:28).

The account then jumps ahead to the meeting between Moses and Aaron and the leaders of Israel in Egypt (4:29–31).

> 7. Read Exodus 4:29–31. In light of their initial response to God, how would you expect the elders of Israel to respond to God from this point forward?

God's people were grateful for God's intervention. But this intervention would not lead to a smooth transition out of Egypt. God was going to allow them to experience some hard circumstances, which would test their trust in Him and try their belief that He is faithful to His promises.

God Allowed Hard Circumstances

Moses and Aaron went in to Pharaoh to communicate to him the demand of the *LORD God* that he let Israel hold a feast to God *in the wilderness* (5:1).

> 8. Read Exodus 5:1, 2. Why would Pharaoh have such a low opinion of Israel's God? Consider Israel's situation.

Moses and Aaron appealed to Pharaoh, saying that God would bring pestilence and sword on Israel if they did not leave to sacrifice to Him. Pharaoh wanted Moses and Aaron to stop encouraging the Israelites to think of such nonsense. He demanded the people get busy building instead (5:4). Furthermore, he took away the straw, making the laborers search for the necessary ingredient for making bricks (5:7). Pharaoh also demanded that the Israelites keep up their pace for making bricks. He figured if they had time to hear tales about their God, then they must be idle and in need of more work (5:8, 9). Letting them take time off would only encourage the Israelites to grow even greater in number.

The Israelites could not keep up their previous pace for producing bricks. As a result, the taskmasters beat the Hebrew officers (5:14). When those officers went to Pharaoh and blamed the Egyptian taskmasters for taking away the straw, Pharaoh again accused Israel of being idle (5:15–18).

The people realized their protests were falling on deaf ears. As they left their meeting with Pharaoh, they met Moses and Aaron, who were waiting to hear the outcome (5:19, 20).

9. Read Exodus 4:31; 5:21. What about God had changed between these two passages?

10. Do a person's circumstances change Who God is? Explain.

Taking his cue from Israel's leaders, Moses went to God to complain. As far as he could see, his appearance before Pharaoh with God's request had triggered disastrous circumstances. Moses asked God why He had brought trouble on the people (5:22). He then went a step further and blamed God for not stepping in to help Israel (5:23). In his estimation, God hadn't done anything at all to deliver His people. Moses basically told God to stop His plan. God was only making things worse.

11. Have you ever felt as if God was being less than faithful? What questions did you want to ask Him?

God was neither absent nor out of control. He went on to communicate to Moses that He would be faithful to His promises.

God Remembered His Covenant

God's answer to Moses could be summed up in one word: *now* (6:1). Moses would begin to see God's hand at work. God would delay His plan no longer. Whether the strong hand in verse 1 refers to Pharaoh or to God is debatable. But either way, God would move to bring about the deliverance of His people.

> 12. Read Exodus 6:2–8. Who is the focus in this passage? How do
>   you know?

God's focus on Himself is further emphasized by the repetition of the phrase *I am the LORD* (6:2, 6, 7, 8). The name *LORD* is *Yahweh*, or *Jehovah*. God had been called by this name as far back as Genesis 4:26. But there was a sense in which the full meaning of that name was not revealed until God began to work on behalf of His people in Egypt (6:3). He was primarily known to the patriarchs as *El Shaddai*, meaning *God Almighty*. As Yahweh/Jehovah, God would be *with* Israel. His *presence* would be particularly evident to them as He brought about their deliverance from Egypt.

God reminded Moses of the covenant He had made with the patriarchs to give them the land in which they sojourned as strangers (6:3, 4). About four hundred years after the patriarchs sojourned in the Promised Land, God heard the groans of His people in Egypt and *remembered* His covenant (6:5). His message to Moses was that He is near and that He is the Covenant Keeper.

God then went on to detail what His covenant keeping would involve so Moses could communicate the details to the Children of Israel (6:6–8). God began this detailing by calling Himself Yahweh again, thus forming the foundation for His actions. He then gave the threefold promise of Israel's deliverance from Egypt (6:6): *I will bring, I will rid*, and *I will redeem*. He spoke as if the action of these verbs had already happened by using a tense that normally indicates past action. God's point was to build Israel's confidence in Him as their Redeemer. Referring to His *stretched out arm* added to the personal, close nature of His redemption of Israel. His use of *arm* was a symbol of His power. And the term *great judgments* meant that God would use the coming plagues to free Israel from Egypt.

God went on to assure Moses, and subsequently Israel, that He would adopt Israel as His own (6:7). That is an amazing truth given Israel's situation at that time.

13. Read Exodus 6:7. What reasons might God have had for choosing another nation to be His people at this point in history?

What God would dare to associate Himself with a nation of poor, dirty, helpless slaves? Yahweh would. He chose to be Israel's God so they could know He is Yahweh, *the LORD*, the God Who is with them and Who would redeem them. Furthermore, Yahweh would give Israel the Promised Land as a heritage, just as He had promised He would (6:8).

When Moses told the Children of Israel all that God was going to do for them, they were not excited or even hopeful (6:9).

14. Read Exodus 6:9. Why didn't Israel trust God?

Israel found no hope in God's message of deliverance. In their estimation, what they were experiencing was too big for God. The weight of the oppression from the Egyptians was affecting them deeply. The language in the passage conveys that they were short of breath in their inner being. In other words, they felt in their souls that they could not catch their breath from sobbing, and some actual sobbing probably did go along with their inward anguish.

Israel's hearts were laid bare by the oppression they were experiencing. Hard circumstances always reveal what is really in a person's heart.

God Used Ordinary People

God's message to Israel was purposefully strong and encouraging. Moses must have originally gone to the Children of Israel with some excitement. But whatever excitement he had felt was soon turned to gloom and doom by the people's doubt. So after God told Moses to speak to Pharaoh (6:10, 11), Moses questioned God once again (6:12). If his own people didn't believe him, how would Pharaoh believe him?

15. Read Exodus 6:13. What did God communicate to Moses by ignoring Moses' objection and charging him and Aaron to bring the Children of Israel out of Egypt?

The text then abruptly transitions to a genealogy. Rather than being out of place, the genealogy serves to contrast Moses and Aaron with Yahweh. Moses and Aaron both descended from Levi, the third son of Jacob (6:18–20). Levi, along with his older brothers Reuben and Simeon, was disqualified from the right of the firstborn (cf. Gen. 34:25–31; 35:22). Remember, that right went to Judah (cf. Gen. 49:8–12). Furthermore, Moses and Aaron weren't even from Levi's oldest son, and Moses was not even the firstborn in his family, since Aaron had been born before him.

The deliverance of Israel was not in human hands; it was in Yahweh's hands (Exod. 6:28, 29). Moses and Aaron had the privilege of being a part of *Yahweh's* work. God graciously included them as His representatives to Pharaoh and the Children of Israel. Moses had trouble seeing that Who God is as Yahweh made his estimation of his own abilities irrelevant (6:30).

God then had a this-is-the-way-it-will-go-down moment with Moses. Moses would be *a god to Pharaoh* and Aaron would be as Moses' *prophet* (7:1). In other words, Moses would speak with all the authority of Yahweh, and Aaron would convey the message to Pharaoh (7:2).

God Restated His Command

God let Moses know up front that he would not be successful in talking to Pharaoh. But Moses' inabilities would not be the reason. God would harden Pharaoh's heart to *multiply* His *signs and . . . wonders* in Egypt (7:3).

16. Read Exodus 7:4, 5. What did God want to teach the Egyptians through the signs and wonders?

The showdown in Egypt was more than just between God and Pharaoh; it was also between God and the Egyptian gods. The next lesson will bear that out. There is some evidence that some of the Egyptians did come to a full realization and acceptance of Israel's God as Yahweh. Apparently some of them left Egypt with the Israelites (12:38).

Perhaps Moses finally understood that resisting God's plan was futile: God had spoken and He would accomplish His plan. Moses and Aaron went to Pharaoh as God had commanded (7:10), performed the signs as

God had prescribed (7:10–12), and got the results that God had predicted (7:13). Yahweh was on the move. The Egyptians' world was about to be rocked to its core. And in the end Yahweh's mighty hand would prevail.

Once the intense persecution came, the people looked at Pharaoh as being too hard to overcome. And Moses consistently considered his own resources as the basis for determining whether he could do what God was asking Him to do.

17. Describe a time when you neglected to do God's will based on the difficulty of your circumstances.

18. Describe a time when you neglected to do God's will based on your estimation of your abilities.

19. What is your estimation of God based on the truths He revealed about Himself in the passage for this lesson?

20. How will you let what you have learned about God affect your willingness to be obedient to Him?

I AM Redeemer

▶ Scripture Focus

Exod. 7:14–12:42

Theme

God is the gracious Redeemer.

> **Memory Verse**
>
> *"And in very deed for this cause have I raised thee up, for to shew in thee my power; and that my name may be declared throughout all the earth" (Exodus 9:16).*

GETTING STARTED

One-of-a-kind items come in just two varieties: those that have monetary value and those that don't. If you have children, you have a lot of the one-of-a-kind items that have little or no monetary value. Yet those might be some of your one-of-a-kind items you value the most.

1. What valuable one-of-a-kind items do you have?

2. What gives them their value?

The Egyptians at the time of the Exodus had identified numerous gods to worship, including several associated with the Nile. God stepped into their pagan world to demonstrate that there is no god like Him in all the earth, a powerful and redeeming one-of-a-kind God.

SEARCHING THE SCRIPTURES

The first nine plagues are neatly arranged in three sets of triplets. Each triplet has a clearly stated purpose. Recognizing those purposes helps us understand God's motivations in bringing the plagues on Egypt.

What is the Redeemer like? God answered that question as He sent the first nine plagues on Egypt. He revealed His power and might. He showed what it means to be Yahweh.

3. Read Psalm 78:40–42. What did the Children of Israel reveal about themselves when they doubted and thereby limited God's power (*hand*)?

First Triplet of Plagues

Moses and Aaron met Pharaoh at the Nile, as God had instructed (7:15). Perhaps Pharaoh was at the river to worship Hapi, the Egyptian god of the Nile. The Nile floodwaters brought fertile soil to Egyptian farmland. The Egyptians believed that without Hapi their nation would die. Hapi's responsibility for sustaining life made him one of the most revered gods in Egypt, perhaps even above Ra, their sun god.

In the setting of the Nile and Egypt's highly revered deity, God revealed His purpose for the first triplet of plagues. He told Pharaoh through Moses and Aaron that the plagues would reveal that He is Yahweh (7:17). Pharaoh would begin to learn about God's character and abilities.

The first plague was the turning of the Nile and other freshwater sources into blood. Even the water the Egyptians had collected in containers turned to blood (7:19). As a result of the plague, the fish in the Nile died; their rotting carcasses created a stench in Egypt (7:21).

Obviously Pharaoh and the rest of Egypt understood that the plague was an attack on their god. The rotten stench was a testimony to Hapi's weakness. Yet Pharaoh's heart was not moved. His magicians duplicated the plague in some way (7:22, 23).

4. Read Exodus 7:24, 25. What did God reveal about His intentions by not changing underground water to blood and by limiting the plague to seven days?

The second plague was the sudden onslaught of frogs. They came from the Nile and filled the land (8:1–6). As with the Nile, the Egyptians saw frogs as sacred.

5. Read Exodus 8:3, 4. How would you respond to having frogs inundate your life?

Though Pharaoh's Egyptians imitated the plague, the constant croaking and the inability to escape the frogs drove Pharaoh to admit the power of Yahweh to take away the frogs (8:7, 8). Moses gave Pharaoh the opportunity to name the time that God would kill the frogs. God responded and killed the frogs the following day as Pharaoh had prescribed (8:9–12). The result was again a stench of rotting flesh throughout the land. But Pharaoh hardened his heart again (8:13–15).

The third plague was turning dust into *lice*, which were possibly gnats or even mosquitos. The plague came without Moses appearing before Pharaoh, and it ended with Pharaoh hardening his heart even more.

6. Read Exodus 8:18, 19. What did the magicians essentially admit about God when they said the plague was His doing?

These first three plagues most likely also came on the Israelites. Those plagues would have helped them understand God's power so they might learn to trust and honor Him.

Second Triplet of Plagues

The purpose of the second set of plagues was to reveal God's providence over the world (8:22). God was in the midst of the land of Egypt even though it was not His *home turf*. His presence and control would be seen as He distinguished between the Israelites and the Egyptians in plagues four through nine.

7. Read Exodus 8:22. When the fourth plague came on only the Egyptians, what explanation for the plagues had to be ruled out?

God presence with Israel was verified by the absence of the plagues in the land of Goshen, where they lived. The Israelites should have felt privileged to be His people.

The second triplet of plagues began with Moses again meeting Pharaoh at the Nile. Moses warned Pharaoh that swarms of flies would inundate the land if he did not let God's people go (8:20, 21). They came as an oppressive swarm and may have been the type of flies that have a painful bite. The flies' presence would have been maddening to the Egyptians.

In response, Pharaoh told Moses to sacrifice to God in the land of Egypt. But doing so would have brought the Egyptians' wrath on the Israelites (8:25, 26). So Pharaoh said he would allow the Israelites to go, but not far away. He then added that he wanted Moses to intercede for him (8:27, 28). Moses said he would intercede for Pharaoh but that Pharaoh should not continue to deal deceitfully with him. God answered Moses' prayer. The flies departed, but Pharaoh hardened his heart again (8:29–32).

The fifth plague was a pestilence on any livestock that remained in the field (9:3). Again God kept the Israelites' livestock safe while also protecting all the livestock the Egyptians brought into shelters (9:4). God showed His power by killing every animal left in the field and by sparing every animal in the shelter. The exact nature of the plague could not be explained as a natural phenomenon.

8. Why might the Egyptians leave their livestock in the field when God gave them an entire day to get the animals to safety?

The specific nature in which this plague was carried out should have been a clue that the plague was not normal. But Pharaoh wanted to be sure. He sent messengers to verify that the Israelites didn't lose any livestock at all (9:7).

9. Read Exodus 9:7. Why would Pharaoh be so interested to know if any of the Israelites' livestock died?

The final plague in the second triplet was the worst yet for the Egyptians physically. Standing in front of Pharaoh, Moses threw ashes from a furnace into the air to cause boils on all the Egyptians and on their livestock (9:8–10). The boils were so painful and debilitating that Pharaoh's magicians were physically unable to stand before him.

10. What did the plague of boils reveal about God's power?

Pharaoh again hardened his heart just as God had said he would (9:11, 12).

Third Triplet of Plagues

God's purpose for bringing the third triplet of plagues on Egypt was to demonstrate that His power is far beyond any other power known to man. God was more powerful than any other god worshiped by anyone on all the earth at that time (9:13, 14). In sending the full furry of His plagues, God would address Pharaoh at his heart. His rebellious, hardened heart would turn to the point of begging the Israelites to leave his land (cf. 6:1).

As Moses met with Pharaoh to start the third set of plagues, God reminded Pharaoh that He could have wiped out the Egyptians. But God had tempered His plagues in order to use Pharaoh to display God's power and to make His reputation and character known worldwide (9:15, 16). Indeed, when the Children of Israel went to enter the Promised Land forty years later, the accounts of the Exodus were still reverberating (cf. Josh. 2:1–11).

11. Read Joshua 2:8–11. How did the account of the Exodus affect the Canaanites?

Since Pharaoh still exalted himself against God's people, God would bring three more devastating plagues on Egypt before the final plague (9:17).

The seventh plague was large hail, heavy rain, and deadly lightning on all those in Egypt who did not seek shelter. The hail was the most devastating hail Egypt had ever experienced (9:18, 24).

12. Read Exodus 9:20, 21. What motivated the Egyptians who called their servants and livestock in from their fields?

Pharaoh initially responded by telling Moses that the Israelites could leave. But as in all the previous plagues, he ended up refusing to let Israel go (9:27–35).

The eighth plague was locust. They finished off the crops that the hail hadn't destroyed. Pharaoh again waffled in his decision about letting Israel go. He even said he had sinned (10:16, 17). But in the end he again hardened his heart (10:20).

The last plague in the third triplet was oppressive darkness that could be *felt* (10:21). No one in Egypt could see anyone else for three days. The nature of the darkness is unknown, though it must have been supernatural, for God again spared Goshen from the plague (10:22, 23). Ra, the Egyptian sun god, would have been humiliated by this plague.

Pharaoh tried to negotiate with Moses but to no avail (10:24–26). Moses would not settle for anything but a complete departure of God's people from the land. Ironically Pharaoh ordered Moses out of his presence, declaring that Moses was to see his face no more. Moses told Pharaoh he would get his wish (10:27–29).

So ended the three triplets of plagues. God had revealed Himself as Yahweh/LORD. His power was evident, as was His mercy. The most severe plagues came with warnings and the means of escaping the consequences of the plagues. A meaningful way of escape came with the tenth plague too.

God Provided Redemption

God first announced the tenth plague to Moses, who then proclaimed it to Pharaoh. Every Egyptian firstborn son and firstborn animal would die in the middle of the night as God passed through Egypt (11:4, 5). The result would be a great cry of grief throughout the land (11:6). But the Israelites would be so peaceful that even dogs wouldn't feel the need to bark. The resultant grief would cause the Egyptians to beg the Israelites to leave their land (11:7, 8).

While communicating the plague to Pharaoh, Moses grew angry with him. Countless lives would be spared if Pharaoh would simply humble himself before God (11:8). But instead Pharaoh remained as hard hearted as ever (11:9, 10).

God gave specific instructions for the first Passover. On the tenth day of the month of the Abib (or Nisan, the current month at that time), each family was to take a year-old, unblemished male lamb and keep it until the fourteenth day (12:1–6). Each family was then supposed to kill their lamb at twilight and to use hyssop (12:22) to apply their lamb's blood to the doorway of their house. The family was to roast the lamb and eat it with unleavened bread and bitter herbs. Each member of the family was to dress as if ready for traveling, even eating with a staff in hand. The uneaten portion of the lamb was to be burned (12:7–11).

When God moved through the land of Egypt, He would kill all the firstborn of all men and beasts that were not under the blood of a passover lamb. By killing both man and beast, God would demonstrate one final time that He was mightier than any god of Egypt represented by the animals and worshiped by men (12:12). The tenth plague was the last in God's blows against the Egyptian deities.

13. Why would it be important for Israel to know that God was far stronger than the gods of the mighty nation of Egypt?

Remember, God protected the Israelites from the effects of plagues four through nine. But with the tenth plague, they needed to carefully follow God's prescribed steps in order to save their firstborn sons alive. The blood applied to their doorways was the sign for God to pass over their household on the night of the plague (12:13). So the lamb took the place of the firstborn son. The lamb was the acceptable substitute for the son.

God did not want Israel to forget their redemption. He instructed them to celebrate Passover every year, repeating some of the elements from the first Passover (12:14). God also gave specific instruction about the Feast of Unleavened Bread, a weeklong observance following the annual celebration of Passover (12:15–20). The Feast of Unleavened Bread was to memorialize how hurriedly the Egyptians made Israel leave their land. And God's emphasis on purity throughout the feast (signified by the absence of leaven in the home) showed the feast's seriousness. The feast was to encourage God's people to increase their faith in God and remind them of His redemption of them.

The Deliverance from Egypt

Moses communicated all of God's instructions to Israel (12:21–27), emphasizing the importance of remembering what God was about to do for them.

14. Read Exodus 12:25–27. What would happen as future generations participated in the passover celebration?

When the people heard all the instructions and how God would spare their firstborn sons, they bowed their heads and worshiped (12:27). The Children of Israel then proceeded to do exactly what God had commanded them to do (12:28).

God passed through Egypt as He had said He would. Every house in Egypt, including Pharaoh's house, experienced a death. The cry that went up in Egypt was great (12:29, 30).

Pharaoh called Moses and Aaron and told them to leave to worship their God (12:31, 32). The rest of Egypt was anxious to get Israel out of their land, fearing they might all die if Israel didn't leave right away. The Children of Israel left with the riches of Egypt, as God had said they would (12:33–36). Apparently some of the Egyptians went with the Israelites, making the group a mixed multitude (12:37, 38).

After 430 years of sojourning, Israel left Egypt on the exact day God had appointed (12:40, 41).

Psalm 105, most likely written by King David, provides additional insight into the Exodus.

15. Read Psalm 105:42, 43. What does David reveal about God's heart during the Exodus?

The blood of the passover lamb is a picture of Christ's shed blood on the cross. Christ purchased our redemption from sin. God was pleased to send His Son to die (Isa. 53:10).

16. Express your gratitude for Christ's death in your place.

17. Who will you tell about the redemption God gladly offers through the blood of Christ?

18. If you were part of Israel at the time of the Exodus, how do you think you would respond to being delivered from Egypt?

19. Does your level of obedience to God match the grandness of your redemption? Explain.

Live in appreciation of the grand redemption God purchased for you. Deliverance from sin should motivate you to obey God more every day.

I AM Leader

▶ Scripture Focus

Exod. 13:17—15:21

Theme

God is worthy of our trust as our leader no matter our circumstances.

Memory Verse

"Who is like unto thee, O LORD, among the gods? who is like thee, glorious in holiness, fearful in praises, doing wonders?"
(Exodus 15:11).

GETTING STARTED

The Battle of Waterloo and the Battle of Little Bighorn were both military disasters. The former was Napoleon's disaster against Anglo-Prussian forces and the latter was Lieutenant Colonel George Custer's disaster against Native Americans. Unfortunately for these military leaders, much of what they accomplished is overshadowed by their disasters.

1. What, if anything, do you associate with Napoleon and Custer more than their military disasters?

2. Why do people tend to remember military leaders primarily for their military disasters?

The account in this study could be called Pharaoh's military disaster. The king of Egypt dared to attack a nation of slaves and lost. This battle helps us understand God's wise and purposeful guidance.

God Led with Wisdom

3. Read Exodus 13:17. What wise decision did God make in leading the Children of Israel?

God knew that when Israel faced an enemy and saw what it meant to battle a well-equipped army, they would turn and run for Egypt. The prospect of having to fight an aggressive foe like the Philistines would have made living in Egypt as a slave an attractive alternative. So God wisely led Israel around by *the way of the wilderness of the Red sea* (13:18). But God wasn't trying to avoid leading His people into the path of an enemy. Instead, God wanted to put the Israelites in a position where *running* was not an option. This became apparent when they reached their destination, which was an unlikely place to camp (14:2).

4. Read Exodus 13:19. What did the long-awaited removal of Joseph's bones from Egypt convey about God?

God visited the Israelites just as Joseph had predicted nearly four hundred years earlier (Gen. 50:25). The long history of God's faithfulness should have encouraged the Israelites as they left Egypt.

5. Read Exodus 13:20–22. Why would God be so visually obvious in leading the Israelites in the way they should go?

God understood the lessons His people needed to learn. And their greatest need after their deliverance from Egypt was to learn to trust Him. So He wisely brought them to a place where they were forced to turn to Him for help.

God Led with Purpose

In relation to Israel, God showed *wisdom* in His leading. In relation to Egypt, He showed *purpose*. He disclosed His purpose for His leading to Moses, who then told the people of Israel (14:1–4). No one was in the dark about God's purpose for His leading.

6. Read Exodus 14:1–4. Why did God lead His people to turn and camp between Migdol and the sea?

Moses related to the people that Pharaoh would think that they had become confused and consequently trapped by the Red Sea. God would then harden his heart to come after the Israelites so God could be victorious over the Egyptians. This was all part of God's larger plan to reveal Himself to Egypt as Yahweh (cf. 7:5, 17; 8:22). Apparently the Israelites went along with it as they followed God to Pi Hahiroth.

As He said He would, God hardened Pharaoh's heart to pursue the Israelites and bring them back to Egypt as slaves. The Israelites would have been vital to Egypt's attempt to recover from the devastating plagues. Pharaoh took all of the chariots he could immediately muster, including his six hundred best, and caught up to the Israelites (14:5–9). The Israelites thought they were trapped and doomed, so they cried out to God (14:10–12).

7. Read Exodus 14:10–12. Would you say Israel's cry to God was based on faith? Explain.

Where was God when Israel cried out to Him and then accused Moses of leading them astray? He was still in *front* of the Israelites in His position as their leader. His role had not changed. The Israelites simply didn't see a way to continue to follow Him because of the Red Sea. Even though God had specifically told them that He would lead them to teach Egypt about His position as Yahweh, the Israelites acted as if God and Moses had lost all control of their lives. They let their limited understanding of their circumstances dictate whether they thought God was trustworthy.

Moses, limited in his understanding of God's plan, told the people not to be afraid and to *stand still, and see the salvation of the LORD* (14:13). Good advice? Yes, except standing still was not part of God's plan. The Lord would *fight* for Israel, but not as they thought He would (14:14). The cloud was still in front of the Children of Israel for a reason. God expected the Israelites to follow Him.

God asked Moses why he cried out to Him as if what to do was not clear. God then simply told Moses to tell the people to *go forward* (14:15). After all, that is where the cloud still resided. *What are you waiting for? Follow Me*, God essentially said. He was still leading them even though they could not yet see the path along the floor of the Red Sea.

> 8. Read Exodus 14:15. How would you have responded to God's instructions to go forward through the Red Sea?

God then told Moses the rest of His plan. He would make a way for the Israelites to follow His lead. Moses was to lift his rod, stretch his hand out over the sea, and divide it so the Children of Israel could cross on dry land. Pharaoh and his army would follow them so God could overcome them (14:16–18).

God Led with Power

The *angel of God* moved to a position of defense (14:19). The identity of the *angel of God* is most likely the divine Angel of the Lord (cf. 3:21). When God moved to behind the Israelites, He provided them with light to see through the night (14:20). God's light illumined the path for the Israelites. In that sense the pillar of fire was still leading the Israelites and showing them where to go. At the same time God caused the pillar of cloud to block out all light for the Egyptians. They couldn't have advanced to engage the Israelites if they had wanted to.

9. What should the people have said to God once He moved to protect them and shed light on the path He had for them?

God used a strong east wind to part the Red Sea, creating a wall of water on both sides of the path through the sea. He also dried out the sea floor making it easier for the Israelites to cross swiftly throughout the night (14:21, 22). How amazed the Israelites must have been to see God's power on display all around them.

Pharaoh directed his army to take the path the Israelites had taken. When his army was between the sea walls, God looked down on him through the pillar of fire and cloud and caused the chariots to bog down and become useless (14:23–25).

10. Read Psalm 77:16–19. What other details does this passage give about God's attack on the Egyptian army in the Red Sea?

11. Read Exodus 14:25. Which direction did the Egyptian army run once they realized God was fighting for Israel?

God instructed Moses to stretch his hand over the sea. Pharaoh's army was crushed under the tremendous speed and weight of the water rushing back to fill the valley God had created in the sea (14:26–28).

12. Read Exodus 14:30, 31. How did God's illustration of His delivering power affect the Israelites?

The crossing of the Red Sea became one of the most referred to events in Israel's history. God used it as a benchmark for His relationship with Israel. It is no wonder that Moses and the Israelites spent time capturing the event in the form of a song. That song reveals the truths they learned about God that day.

13. What two truths about God might you put into a song about His deliverance of Israel from the Egyptian army?

Israel learned that God is strong, unmatched, and able to carry out His promises. They burst forth in a song of praise to God.

God Is Strong and Unmatched

The first part of Moses' song looks back at what God had just done for Israel (15:1–12). That section of the song includes two full strophes and part of another. The first strophe (15:1b–5) begins with a confession about God. Though all of Israel was singing the song, each individual sang from his personal perspective and communicated his confession directly with God (15:1, 2).

The Israelites understood God's role as their strength and protection. They also understood that God had been fulfilling this role since the time of their fathers, a reference to the patriarchs (15:2).

14. Read Exodus 15:2. What were some of the implications of each Israelite recognizing God as his personal God?

The people picked up on the importance of the name *Yahweh* in their song (15:3). God had emphasized His name throughout His interaction with them and the Egyptians (cf. 7:5, 17; 8:22). As a result of God's actions, they believed He would be near them and would be active in their lives.

The first strophe ends with a narration of what God did to the Egyptian army (15:4, 5). As Yahweh, God drowned Pharaoh's army, making the soldiers sink to *the bottom as a stone.*

The second strophe (15:6–10) continues a reflection on what God had just done for Israel. God's *right hand* is a central focus of this strophe. God's *right hand* is a poetic way of referring to His *omnipotence*. God can do whatever He pleases with His *right hand*. As the Israelites observed God's actions, God's *right hand* became *glorious in power*, meaning it became illustrative of what God is capable of doing. Specifically, the Lord *dashed in pieces the enemy* (15:6). The crushing weight of the water returning to its normal depth probably would have been strong enough to tear the bodies of the Egyptian soldiers apart. When the soldiers rose up against the Lord, God tore them down in the greatness of His majesty and consumed them by His wrath (15:7).

> 15. Suppose two people are fighting. One can use his hands to fight, while the other is limited to breathing air through his nose as his offensive attack. What would you predict would happen?

Moses helped convey the ridiculousness of the Egyptian army's claims. Egypt had said the soldiers would destroy Israel with their hands. But God defeated them so easily that it was as if He simply used the breath of His nostrils to win the fight (15:8–10). God's *breath* is a reference to the mighty wind that divided the Red Sea and then caused it to return to normal (cf. 14:21).

Based on God's defeat of the Egyptian army with just His breath, the third strophe (15:11–16a) begins with a rhetorical question: *Who is like unto thee, O LORD, among the gods?* The understood answer is *no one.*

> 16. Read Exodus 15:11. Why was it so important for Israel to know that there was no other god like Yahweh?

God's *holiness* is what made Him different from all the other gods (15:11). As holy, He always does what is right. So Israel could always trust Him. They did not have to worry that one day God would turn evil and destroy them without a just cause. Other nations had gods that required child sacrifices in order to be appeased. Of course all those gods were false. But the anxiety felt by those who worshiped those gods was real.

The third strophe includes another reference to God's hand (15:12). God extended it, and the earth swallowed up the Egyptians. The rest of the third strophe looks forward to God's future dealings with Israel.

God Is Able to Fulfill His Promises

Israel stood on the east side of the Red Sea. Their ties with Egypt had been cut. There was no easy path back. God wanted the sea as a barrier between them and Egypt to help the Israelites think about their future in the Promised Land instead of their past in Egypt.

The third strophe continues by declaring that God would successfully lead the Israelites to the Promised Land, called the *holy habitation* (15:13). The crossing of the Red Sea made Israel confident that the Lord would guide them, His redeemed, by His mercy and strength (15:13). Such confidence in the Lord's leading emboldened the Israelites. Instead of cowering from the prospect of fighting the Philistines (cf. 13:17), they said the Philistines would be the ones anguishing once the report of the Red Sea crossing spread (15:14). The same would hold for the chiefs of Edom, the mighty men of Moab, and the inhabitants of Canaan. They would be dismayed, tremble, and melt away as they faced the greatness of God's arm (15:15, 16).

The comparison of Israel's enemies to a stone marks the end of the third strophe. The first two strophes also ended with a mention of rock or lead (15:5, 10). The fourth strophe continues Israel's prospect of crossing over to the Promised Land as God's redeemed (15:16b). Israel's hope for entering and taking the Promised Land rested fully on the Lord. Verse 17 lists all that the Lord would do to make possession of the land possible. That anticipation of God's leadership in bringing Israel into the land is right on. Psalm 44 gives the perspective of Israelites in the land long after it had been conquered. It affirms what was still a hope in Exodus 15:17.

17. Read Psalm 44:1–8. What message about the conquest of the Promised Land did the forefathers pass on to future generations?

The Promised Land was not only for Israel, but it was also the place God would choose to dwell with men (Exod. 15:17). At first He did so in the tabernacle and then in the temple. Eventually Christ will reign on earth during the Millennium (cf. Rev. 20:4). And finally Christ will reign forever in the presence of all the redeemed on a new earth (cf. Rev. 21:22–27). Truly *the Lord shall reign for ever and ever* (Exod. 15:18).

Both the interlude of narrative (15:19) and Miriam's song (15:21) recap what the Lord did for Israel. The focus is on the Lord's work. Miriam's song was sung by women as an antiphonal response, meaning they sung the song at the end of each strophe.

MAKING IT PERSONAL

All believers have God in them in the Person of the Holy Spirit, a much better Guide than a pillar of cloud and fire. The Holy Spirit can convict, assure, strengthen, and enable us. We become more attentive to the Spirit's leading when we spend time in His Word and in prayer.

18. How aware are you of the Spirit's leading in your life?

19. What could you do to sharpen your attention to His leading?

20. When have you complained to God about your circumstances?

21. What might *going forward* look like in your situation?

I AM Provider

▶ Scripture Focus

Exod. 15:22—17:16

Theme

God wants us to humble ourselves before Him and trust Him to provide for our needs in His time.

Memory Verse

"Do all things without murmurings and disputings: That ye may be blameless and harmless, the sons of God, without rebuke, in the midst of a crooked and perverse nation, among whom ye shine as lights in the world" (Philippians 2:14, 15).

GETTING STARTED

Every day we are bombarded with ads that point out our problems and then present us with solutions. We can control the color of our teeth and hair and make our paunch disappear, or so we are led to believe. The products are part of a growing trend to try to control every aspect of our lives.

1. If you were in charge of all the circumstances surrounding your life, what circumstances from this past week would you have changed?

2. What might be some indicators that a person wishes he was in charge of all the circumstances of his life?

The Israelites expected God to make their lives comfortable after they left Egypt and crossed the Red Sea. Instead, God repeatedly led them to places where they suffered need. Their responses to their needs exposed their power struggle against God. This study will help you see your need to humble yourself before God and to trust Him to provide for your needs in His time.

Perhaps the Israelites thought life would never be hard again after Egypt. They praised God for how He delivered them from Pharaoh's army. But their praise was not an indication that Israel was fully devoted to following Him. God had some tests for Israel that would reveal the true nature of their hearts.

Test at Marah

Moses led Israel into the wilderness of Shur, heading south along the Gulf of Suez for three days. They didn't find any drinking water along the way (15:22). Eventually they came to Marah, probably modern-day Ain Hawarah, where they found undrinkable, bitter water (15:23).

Going without water for three days, finding water, and then discovering that the water is undrinkable is hard to handle both physically and emotionally. The Israelites asked Moses, *What shall we drink?* That is a legitimate question. But Israel murmured as they asked the question.

3. Read Exodus 15:24. Why is whining a sin?

4. Why do hardships often cause people to complain against God?

When God brought the Israelites out of Egypt, His goal wasn't to make their lives comfortable. Instead He wanted them to have a heart for Him. So He led them to places of need on purpose. The needs exposed their true nature.

5. Read Deuteronomy 8:2, 3. What did God want the Israelites to learn?

It is ironic that Israel worried about having no drinking water just days after God had used millions of gallons of water to utterly destroy Egypt's army. God had demonstrated His absolute power over nature; they had even sung about it. In addition, they had witnessed God turn the Nile River into blood. If God displayed the power to do such grand miracles in nature, then He could certainly change bitter water into drinking water.

Moses heard the people's murmuring and turned to God for help. God showed Moses a tree and told him to throw it into the well to make the water palatable (15:25a). Notice that God was patient with Israel. He didn't jump on them for their lack of faith. He didn't go into a tirade about how much He had done for them to get them to Marah. He was very gracious to them, providing for their needs despite their murmuring.

God Gave an Ordinance

After graciously providing water for His people, God made a *statute and an ordinance* for Israel (15:25b, 26). The statute and ordinance would *test* the Israelites and reveal their hearts as they journeyed through the wilderness.

6. Read Exodus 15:25b, 26. What would Israel need to believe about God in order to obey His voice?

7. What reasons did Israel have for believing that God was the one true God Who stays true to His word?

God's ordinance was a conditional promise. If they were diligent to heed God's voice, obey Him, and keep all His statutes, then God would not put on them any of the *diseases* He had put on the Egyptians. The mention of *diseases* is not a general reference to illnesses of any kind. God did not promise Israel perfect health if they obeyed Him. The word *diseases* probably included the plagues God had brought on the Egyptians, especially the boils, as well as any other disease God intentionally used to chasten His people (Deut. 28:27–29, 60, 61). The conditional promise is that God would refrain from sending devastating, widespread diseases on Israel if they observed His commands.

8. Read Deuteronomy 28:58–61. What would be some indicators that God was chastening His people with diseases?

God then identified Himself as the LORD *that healeth thee* (Exod. 15:26) in the sense that if Israel responded to His chastening, He would remove the diseases He had brought on them as a result of their disobedience.

God brought the plagues on Egypt so Pharaoh would let God's people go. But He also brought them to address Egypt's refusal to acknowledge that all their blessings had come from Him rather than from their false gods. God clearly said that He wanted Egypt to know Him as Yahweh (cf. 7:5, 17; 8:22). Consequently all of the plagues directly affected either Egypt's abundance or its well-being. And all of the plagues challenged Egypt's gods. Yet most of the Egyptians defied God. They refused to recognize Yahweh as the One Who had blessed their land so richly. Israel then witnessed the subsequent devastation.

God wanted Israel to rely on Him for their needs. Having them witness the plagues and travel through the wilderness would show them that He was reliable and trustworthy. Once they settled in the Promised Land, they would have an abundance of food and water. They would become like the Egyptians with good cropland and many natural resources. Their temptation in the Promised Land would not be to complain about a lack of food or water; their temptation would be to serve and credit other gods for all the abundance *God* had provided for them. God warned Israel not to let that happen (Duet. 4:15–24; 12:29–32).

9. Read Deuteronomy 28:45–47. What did God expect from Israel once they were in the Promised Land?

God went on to warn Israel about failing to obey and serve Him (Duet. 28:49–57). If they did, another nation would invade them, eat their crops, and consume their abundance. Israel would be left without any food at all. In fact, they would become so desperate while under siege that they would eat their own children. Once in captivity they would be hungry, thirsty, and lacking their basic needs (28:48). Israel didn't heed these warnings once they were in the Promised Land. Both Israel and Judah were eventually taken into captivity by Assyria and Babylon respectively.

Whether Israel worshiped God in the Promised Land would partly depend on whether they humbled themselves to trust God to provide for their needs. So it makes sense that God began Israel's journey through the wilderness at

Marah where He exposed their lack of trust in Him and their thirst for control over their own lives. He wanted them to turn to Him and worship Him as their provider of needs even in the midst of their needs. They wanted a god whom they could control and to whom they could dictate. They wanted to serve a god who would never lead them to a place of need.

10. Read Exodus 15:27. How would you expect Israel to respond to God for leading them to Elim, a place with plenty of drinking water?

There is no record of Israel saying thanks to God for the provision of water at Elim (15:27). That would have been the right response. If they had rejoiced in the Lord, no doubt Moses would have included that in his record, especially sandwiched between such glaring examples of a lack of trust in God.

11. What is true of the hearts of those who fail to thank God for providing for their needs?

Test in the Desert of Sin

After God's provision of water at Marah and Elim, we might expect the Israelites to respond to God with trust the next time they had a need.

God tested Israel again in the Wilderness of Sin between Elim and Mount Sinai. The entire congregation complained to Moses and Aaron, saying it would have been better if the Lord had killed them in Egypt, where at least they had meat and bread to eat (16:1–3). How silly to prefer a full belly over life! But that is a testimony to how much Israel wanted to control God and have Him bend to their dictates.

Israel obviously had selective memory. They remembered only that they had had full bellies in Egypt. They forgot that they were worked to the point of exhaustion. They forgot about the unrealistic demands the Egyptians put on them. Or how the Egyptians killed their firstborn boys. They forgot they were slaves! And even more unbelievably, they were ungrateful for all the miracles God had wrought to free them from slavery. Had Israel's heart changed? No.

God patiently provided for the Israelites again. He rained down bread, called manna, for them to gather in the morning. In the evening He brought quail for them to catch and eat.

Moses and Aaron were careful to point out to the Israelites that their complaints were against God (16:7, 8). They were right in doing so. The Israelites should have recognized just how offensive their complaining was to God.

Through this provision of food God expected His people to know that He is the LORD *your God* (16:12). As such, He should have been responded to with humility and worship (cf. Deut. 8:2, 3). Instead they maintained their desire for God to serve them according to their wishes.

God Gave Limitations

Along with the provision of food, God gave specific regulations to test the Israelites to see if they would obey Him. The first regulation was simple: God forbade Israel from leaving any leftover manna in their tents overnight. If they did, the manna would stink and be filled with worms. Acting like toddlers who disobey despite clear instructions, some of the Israelites kept leftovers overnight. They awoke to the rank smell of rotting manna.

12. Read Exodus 16:19–21. Why would God want the Israelites to throw out their leftovers every evening?

This blatant disobedience showed that Israel was in a power struggle with God for control of their circumstances. So they tested Him by collecting more manna than He had commanded them to collect.

God's second regulation seemed to violate His first one. On the sixth day of the week the Israelites were to gather twice as much manna so they would have something to eat on the Sabbath (16:22–26). Not surprisingly some of the Israelites went hungry on the Sabbath (16:27). Again, they wanted God to serve them and conform to their desires.

The Lord asked Moses how long the people would refuse to keep His commandments, clearly indicating their problem was a heart problem. The people rebelled against God by *purposefully* disobeying His regulations. Lack of communication was not the problem; hunger and thirst for power was.

The provision of manna was a watershed moment for Israel and their relationship with God. It proved that God would care for their daily needs. God instructed Moses to gather some of the manna and keep it as a testimony of His faithfulness to Israel in the wilderness. Future generations would observe the manna and know that God is the provider of needs (16:32–36).

Test at Rephidim

By now we might expect Israel to be ready to humbly submit to God. After all, they are getting bread and meat every day. God tested them one more time to see what their hearts might reveal.

The Israelites set out from the Wilderness of Sin and came to Rephidim where they found no water to drink.

13. Read Exodus 17:1–4. What evidence is there that the Israelites actually trusted God less at Rephidim?

The people's complaints at Rephidim provided the third witness about the condition of their hearts. They wanted God to conform to their desires and to follow their timing.

Once again, God provided water for the Israelites. Moses took the rod he used to turn the Nile into blood and struck a rock. God caused water to flow from the rock so Israel could quench their thirst (17:5–7).

The last statement of verse 7 is very telling: *they tempted the LORD, saying, Is the LORD among us, or not?* (17:7). By this question about God's presence, the Israelites again revealed that they expected God to serve them according to their expectations of Him. Their needs made them question God's presence. They expected God to provide for their needs instantly and according to their liking. They would have learned this expectation from watching the Egyptians interact with their gods. The Egyptians conducted themselves in such a way as to try to control and coerce their gods in order to have comfortable, easy lives. But God cannot be controlled and coerced. The three tests in the wilderness revealed Israel's lack of humility before Him.

14. Based on Israel's short track record in the wilderness, would you say they deserved to be delivered from Egypt? Explain.

15. Why would God deliver such a rebellious, hard-hearted, doubtful, demanding, power-hungry people from slavery?

God established that Israel was rebellious and power hungry. His next stop in leading His people would be Mount Sinai, the place where He would continue to reveal Himself to His people by illustrating His holiness and by giving them a law to obey.

MAKING IT PERSONAL

If people were able to run their lives, they would make sure they never felt a need or went without. With that expectation as part of their thinking, they are tempted to conclude that there is something wrong with God when they do have a need. Complaining reveals a lack of trust in God as well as a lack of humble submission to Him.

16. What circumstances do you find yourself complaining about?

17. What is the root cause of your complaints? What does your complaint reveal about your relationship with God?

Our greatest need is never the emptiness of our wallets or our stomachs; it is always what is lacking in our hearts. Our needs present us with opportunities to humble ourselves before God and to declare our trust in Him, trusting in God's grace to sustain us and in His wisdom to guide us.

18. Ask God to help you trust Him in the midst of your needs.

19. Praise God for His sustaining grace and guidance in the midst of your needs.

I AM Instructor

▶ Scripture Focus

Exod. 19:1—20:21

Theme

God is the source of direction on how to live rightly before Him.

> ### Memory Verses
>
> *"Ye have seen what I did unto the Egyptians, and how I bare you on eagles' wings, and brought you unto myself. Now therefore, if ye will obey my voice indeed, and keep my covenant, then ye shall be a peculiar treasure unto me above all people: for all the earth is mine" (Exodus 19:4, 5).*

GETTING STARTED

Oops! I should have read the directions! So say those who act first and read the directions only if problems arise. Pouring bleach and ammonia together sounds like a great idea for example. You get the disinfecting power of bleach with the cutting power of ammonia. But the directions say don't do it. The mixture gives off deadly fumes!

1. How often do you stop to read the directions on a product?

2. When have you had a problem arise because you failed to read the directions?

God called Israel out of Egypt and made them His own. Shortly thereafter He gave them *instructions for use* and *warnings* so they could live in accordance with His desires. This study will examine the Ten Commandments, the most famous section of God's instructions for Israel's life after redemption.

God's Covenant with Israel

Exodus 19:4–6 is the Sinaitic/Mosaic Covenant between God and Israel. The covenant is conditional and temporal rather than unconditional and permanent like the Noahic (Gen. 9:8–17) and Abrahamic (12:1–3) Covenants.

Moses delivered God's message to the nation. It began with a summary of God's working with Israel so far. God used the image of a mother eagle encouraging her eaglets to get out of the nest and fly (Exod. 19:4). In creation a mother eagle will stir up the nest and force her eaglets to learn to fly by carrying them on her wings. The eagle protects her young from falling until they are able to soar on their own.

In a sense Egypt was the Israelites' *nest.* They faced hardships in Egypt, but they had their needs for food, water, and shelter met without interruption. God took the initiative to lead them out of their nest to force them to fly.

3. Why else might Israel long for Egypt when they faced tough circumstances?

During their journey to the Promised Land, Israel longed for Egypt when life got hard, resenting God and questioning His motives (16:3). The Israelites needed to learn to follow God's instructions for life. They needed to mature in their faith and learn to trust the Lord.

God's Conditions and Blessings

God continued His message to Israel by sharing three benefits the people would realize if they obeyed Him and kept His covenant with them. God said Israel would become *a peculiar treasure, a kingdom of priests,* and *an holy nation* (19:5, 6).

4. Read Exodus 19:5. What did Israel know about being treated as a special treasure by other nations? Consider what life was like for Israelites in Egypt.

God chose Israel to be His special *treasure*. That means Israel was valuable to God and that He had a purpose for the nation. But it was not as if God had to settle for Israel, a lowly people the other nations would have considered as a commodity rather than a nation. God could have selected any nation to be His people. After all, as their creator He owns all of them. God chose Israel over even Egypt with all of its brilliant gold, massive structures, strong army, superior intellect, and incredible wealth. What a privilege and a responsibility for Israel.

Israel could also become a *kingdom of priests*. God intended for every Israelite to show God's truth and blessings to the other nations. Other nations would learn about God and His blessings through Israel as God's people lived for Him. Serving other gods and worshiping idols, however, would destroy Israel's role as a kingdom of priests.

Finally, Israel had the opportunity to become a *holy nation*. To be *holy* means to be *set apart*. Israel was to be set apart to the Lord. God gave Israel specific instructions on what that set-apart-life would look like. As the people lived set apart to God, they would reflect His holiness.

5. Read Leviticus 11:44, 45; 20:26. Why did God want Israel to be holy?

Israel was freed from Egypt, but they belonged to God. That meant they weren't free to do whatever they pleased. That actually would not have been freedom at all.

6. Why is being free to do whatever you desire not true freedom?

The Israelites didn't free themselves of a master when they left Egypt; they simply changed masters. God was their new master.

Israel as a whole responded to God's words. They said, *All that the* Lord *hath spoken we will do* (Exod. 19:8). Since God had spoken only in generalities about His commands, Israel didn't see a reason for not agreeing to follow what He said. Little did they know that His law would be specific and life-encompassing. As immature people with a full understanding of neither God's character and ways nor their own limitations and sinfulness, the Israelites thought they could live in obedience to God. Their failures over the few months since leaving Egypt should have been clues to their inability to obey God without hesitation. Most likely their own impressions of what it would mean to obey God clouded their understanding of what obedience to God would actually require.

God's Stipulations for Covenant Blessing

After hearing Moses' report about the people's response, God told Moses He was coming to him in a thick cloud and speaking so the people would be able to hear Him. The primary reason for this setup was to cause the people to believe Moses' words (19:9). It would be clear that the law was from God's mouth rather than Moses' mouth.

God instructed Moses in how the people were supposed to prepare for God's arrival on Mount Sinai. Moses was to consecrate the people and then have them wash their clothes (19:10). The removal of dirt would be respectful of God's holiness and illustrate their need to be clean, or holy, at the heart level when God arrived on the third day (19:11).

Moses was to set up a barrier around the base of the mountain to keep the people from even touching the mountain. Those who touched the mountain were to be put to death. God prescribed stones and arrows as the means of execution so the executioners would not have to touch the defiled violators' bodies. The long trumpet sound was the signal for the people to come near the mountain and for Moses to ascend it (19:12, 13).

Moses returned to the people and communicated all God's instructions, adding that husbands were not to go near their wives for the three days prior to God's arrival (19:14, 15). The mandatory abstinence was a matter of further consecration.

God arrived in a dramatic way, with thundering and lightning, a thick cloud, and a very loud trumpet. The people trembled (19:16, 17) and moved away from the mountain. They asked Moses to speak with them instead of God, fearing they would die if God spoke to them (20:18, 19). Moses, trembling himself at the coming of the Lord on the mountain (cf. Heb. 12:21), told the people not to fear death. God had come to test them and to teach them to respect Him (Exod. 20:20, 21).

Moses obediently ascended the mountain at God's request. Once Moses was there, God told him to return to the people and warn them once again about not breaking through the barrier to touch the mountain. Surprisingly, Moses questioned the necessity of warning the people once again. God insisted, so Moses went and did as He had said (19:21–25).

7. Why would God insist on Moses returning to warn the people a second time?

The three days of preparation, the washing of their clothes, the barrier on the mountain, the warnings, and the majestic arrival of the Lord on the mountain must have impressed on the Israelites that they were not like God. He is holy, and they were sinful.

God's Law

God gave the beginning of His law to Moses. The distance between Mount Sinai and the Children of Israel apparently kept the Israelites from hearing God give the law to Moses well enough to understand it. Moses later declared it to them (cf. Deut. 5:4, 5). The fact that *God* gave the instructions on how to live properly before Him is important.

God's laws provided the primary stipulations for the Mosaic Covenant. As mentioned, the Mosaic Covenant was conditional and temporal. If Israel wanted God's blessings, then Israel was required to keep the laws. The Ten Commandments (cf. 5:7–21), written on the two tables of stone by God Himself (Exod. 24:12; 31:18; 34:28), provided the heart of these covenantal requirements. The rest of the law (Exod. 20—40; Lev. 1—27; Num. 1:1—10:10) provided additional requirements. The laws, then, are not requirements for us as New Testament believers because we are not partners in the Mosaic Covenant. Besides, the old Mosaic Covenant is no longer operative (Heb. 8:6–13).

It should also be noted that keeping the Ten Commandments or any of the other parts of the law had nothing to do with salvation for the Israelites. Salvation has always been through faith, as it was with Abraham, who lived before the law of Moses (cf. Gen. 15:1–6).

The Ten Commandments breaks into two sections. The first four commands have to do with Israel's relationship with God. The last six commands have to do with Israel's relationship with others.

Israel's Relationship with God

The first command begins with a reminder that God brought Israel out of Egypt, the *house of bondage* (20:2). This act of redemption was the basis for God's covenant with Israel. Obedience to the law was to be a response to God's redemption. So it makes sense that the Ten Commandments begin with God and how Israel was to live in relationship to Him. Israel was foremost not to have any other gods before God.

The second command prohibited the making of idols and bowing to them. God said He is a jealous God and would not tolerate any idol worship.

8. Read Exodus 20:4–6. What was the connection between God's jealousy and His love for His people?

Idol worship brought consequences on God's people. Those consequences could be felt for several generations. God wanted to bless His people instead of seeing them experience the consequences of idolatry.

The third command forbade taking the name of the Lord God in vain (20:7). God's name stood for His reputation. Israel was not to use God's name dishonestly, such as in conjunction with a promise a person didn't intend to keep (cf. Lev. 19:12). Taking God's name in vain would also include using it for selfish reasons or personal gain.

The fourth command was to remember the Sabbath day *to keep it holy* (Exod. 20:8). The Israelites kept the Sabbath *holy* by approaching the day differently than the rest of the week, treating it as a day to the Lord. No one, including servants and animals, was to work on the Sabbath (20:9, 10).

The pattern for Israel's week is based on God's six days of creative work and His one day of rest (20:11). So observing the Sabbath was a weekly reminder of God's work in creation. The Sabbath was also connected to the Exodus and served as a reminder of God's deliverance of Israel (Deut. 5:15).

9. Why would it be important for Israel to remember God's creation week?

10. What three words would you use to summarize Israel's relationship with God based on the first four commands?

11. What did God reveal about Himself through the first four commands?

Israel's Relationship with Others

The rest of the commands regulated relationships among the Israelites. The fifth command is the only positively stated command of the remaining six. It is also the only one in the second set that is accompanied by a promise.

12. Read Exodus 20:12. Why would honoring their parents lead to a long sojourn in the Promised Land?

The sixth command prohibited murder. This command was not a restriction on killing in general. The Israelites had already fought and defeated the Amalekites under God's direction (17:13), killing them with the sword. Self-defense and capital punishment are also not included in this command. The restriction was on taking someone's life unjustly. All human life is valuable, because every person is made in God's image (Gen. 9:6).

The seventh command told the Israelites not to commit adultery (Exod. 20:14). God took a high view of the marriage relationship and the home in general by naming adultery as a capital crime (Lev. 20:10).

13. Why would strong marriages have been important for Israel's future?

A husband and wife made their marriage commitment before God. So committing adultery against one's spouse was also breaking one's commitment to God.

The eighth command prohibited stealing (Exod. 20:15). When an Israelite stole something, he was communicating to God either that he was not satisfied with what God had given him or that he didn't think he could find complete satisfaction in his relationship with God. Either way, stealing was highly offensive to God. Furthermore, God had given each Israelite all he had. To steal was to take what God had personally given to someone else.

Telling a lie against a neighbor was prohibited in the ninth command (20:16). God actually required witnesses in a murder trial to also be the executioners (Deut. 17:6–13), making it far less likely that a witness would lie against the defendant.

The final directive was a command against coveting (Exod. 20:17). An Israelite was not to covet his neighbor's house, wife, servants, animals, or anything else that belonged to his neighbor. Like stealing, coveting is an expression of dissatisfaction with how God has blessed people. The covetous person believes he could distribute blessings better than God. Contentment is the opposite of covetousness.

14. What three words would you use to summarize Israel's relationship with one another based on the final six commands?

15. What did God reveal about Himself through the final six commands?

The Ten Commandments bring guilt. Jesus made this even clearer when He pointed out that the person who hates someone is guilty of murder and the man with lustful thoughts is guilty of adultery (Matt. 5:21, 22, 27, 28). While the Ten Commandments show a person that he is sinful, they are powerless to solve the sin problem. But praise God for salvation from your sins! Through Christ your guilt is all gone. You stand righteous before the Lord.

The Ten Commandments are not for believers today. They were specifically for Israel as stipulations for the Mosaic Covenant. Nine of the commandments are repeated in some form in the New Testament, but not as stipulations for receiving God's blessings. The church obeys God's commands in the New Testament out of love and gratitude for God. This is called grace living. God has been faithful to provide for us in the New Testament all the directives we need for living pleasing to Him by His grace (2 Peter 1:2–4).

16. Why do you obey God?

17. How might obeying God out of love and gratitude for Him change your perspective on your relationship with God?

I AM
Glorious God

▶ Scripture Focus

Exod. 24:1—34:28

Theme

God is glorious in His justice, mercy, and grace in His dealings with humanity.

Memory Verse

"And the LORD passed by before him, and proclaimed, The LORD, The LORD God, merciful and gracious, longsuffering, and abundant in goodness and truth, keeping mercy for thousands, forgiving iniquity and transgression and sin, and that will by no means clear the guilty" (Exodus 34:6, 7a).

GETTING STARTED

We all have inglorious moments. Some of them we stumble into because of our carelessness. Falling flat on your face at a public event is embarrassing, but it doesn't take long to recover from such an inglorious moment. Other inglorious moments are far more serious.

1. When has your carelessness caused an inglorious moment for you?

2. What do you learn about people from their responses to their inglorious moments?

This study covers how God used a rather inglorious moment in Israel's history to reveal to them His glory.

Ratification of the Covenant

God instructed Moses and his aides to come up to Him on Mount Sinai. But first they were to meet with Israel to ratify the covenant (24:1, 2). Moses communicated all the Lord's words and all His judgments (24:3). The people responded again with one voice saying, *All the words which the LORD hath said will we do*. Moses recorded all the words of the Lord and made an altar at the foot of Sinai. He also set up twelve pillars, one for each of the tribes of Israel (24:4). The *young men* Moses sent to offer burnt offerings and sacrifice peace offerings were firstborn sons who played the roles of priests until the Aaronic priesthood was in place (24:5).

Moses proceeded to officially ratify the covenant. He collected half of the blood from the sacrifices and put it in basins. He sprinkled blood on the altar and read the book of the covenant to the people. They again agreed to do all that God had commanded (24:6, 7). Moses continued the ratification process by sprinkling the people with some of the blood as a blood oath, meaning the people were bound to obey the Lord (24:8). The blood on the altar was a symbol of God's acceptance of the offering and the forgiveness He granted as a result. This prefigured Christ's shed blood on behalf of humanity (cf. Heb. 9:11–15).

3. How would you describe Israel's relationship with God at this time?

Moses and his aides, including Joshua, ascended Mount Sinai to meet with the Lord. As they went, they witnessed an appearance by God. They saw a glimpse of God standing on sapphire that was so pure it appeared to be something from Heaven (24:9, 10).

4. Read Exodus 24:9, 10. How might you expect God's appearance to affect Aaron's understanding of God?

The men responded to God's revelation of His glory by eating a meal together, a common occurrence for the ratification of a covenant in those days (24:11).

God then called Moses and Joshua to go higher on the mountain, leaving the elders with Aaron and Hur. Moses eventually left Joshua, too, as he continued on up the mountain to meet with the Lord and receive the tablets on which God had written the Ten Commandments (24:12–15). After six days, the Lord called to Moses out of the cloud that accompanied His presence. To the people at the base of Mount Sinai, God's glory appeared on the mountain as a consuming fire (24:16–18; cf. 19:18).

5. What did God reveal about Himself by appearing to Israel as a consuming fire?

God's Dwelling Place

God's plans for the tabernacle dominated His new revelation to Moses. The tabernacle was where God planned to dwell with Israel. Given its importance, God gave Moses specific instructions on how to build the tabernacle and what furniture to put in it.

6. Read Exodus 25:21, 22. Why was the mercy seat so important?

The ark of the covenant was the place of atonement. Israel was accepted by God as a result of a substitute sacrifice. Their sins were covered, albeit temporarily. The sacrifices had to continue year after year. This temporary atonement for sins was a precursor to Christ's final sacrifice for sins on the cross (Heb. 10:11, 12).

7. Read Exodus 25:40; 26:30. How important were the details God spelled out for Moses on Mount Sinai?

God was so specific about the tabernacle because it was Israel's means of approaching Him. Israel was to approach Him according to *His* plan. God's communication of all the details was part of the reason Moses spent so much time on the mountain.

God ended His instructions on the tabernacle by repeating His command about keeping the Sabbath (31:12–18). He reminded Moses about the connection between the Sabbath and God's week of creation (31:17). That connection reminded Moses and eventually Israel that they served the creator of the universe.

After noting that God inscribed the Ten Commandments on two tablets and gave them to Moses (31:18), the narrative switches to what Israel was doing at the base of Mount Sinai.

Israel's Rejection of the Covenant

Moses had been away for forty days with no word on why he had been gone so long. The Israelites grew impatient. The Israelites saw the time as an indication of Moses' failure and God's apparent absence (32:1).

8. Read Exodus 32:1. What might you conclude about Israel's belief in God, based on their decision to make an idol?

It is hard to imagine how Israel could decide to make a god after witnessing all God had done for them. It shows how prone their hearts were to wander.

9. Read Exodus 25:1–3, 8; 32:2, 3. What similarities do you notice in these verses?

Aaron fashioned a gold calf with an engraving tool and presented it to the people as the god that had brought them out of Egypt (32:4). The calf was a sign of strength and fertility. So Aaron was reshaping Israel's understanding of God. He made an image to represent God and built an altar to worship the image. Aaron then proclaimed the next day as a feast day to the Lord (32:5). By doing so, Aaron claimed authority on how to worship the Lord. Following Aaron's lead, the people claimed authority to determine worship rituals too.

The next day all of Israel rose early and offered burnt offerings and peace offerings. They then sat down to eat and drink. But this was no church potluck. The Israelites indulged their fleshly desires. The word *play* (32:6) can refer to *conjugal caresses*, perhaps indicating an improper sexual element. Their worship was grotesque, a drunken orgy.

Israel already had the Ten Commandments. Those laws represented God's authority over them. By violating the second commandment, they were in essence rejecting God and His authority to order their lives. They no doubt thought such an arrangement would bring them endless freedom and frivolity. But they didn't understand that embracing idolatry was to embrace slavery to sin.

Moses' Appeal to God's Mercy

Back on the mountain, Moses was standing with the Ten Commandments in his hands when God gave him an urgent command: *Go, get thee down!* (32:7). The Israelites had corrupted themselves, and Moses needed to address the problem right away.

God told Moses what Israel had done. He called the Israelites *stiffnecked* (32:9), meaning they refused to submit to His leadership. By contrast Israel was so eager to worship their idol and bow to its authority that they got up early in the morning to get a head start (32:6).

10. Read Exodus 32:10. How serious was Israel's sin?

Motivated by His justice, God told Moses to let Him alone so He might consume the Israelites in His wrath and raise up a great nation from Moses (32:10). Moses boldly interceded for the Israelites, appealing to God's mercy. Moses argued that Egypt would think God had brought His people into the wilderness just to kill them. Furthermore, God had promised the patriarchs that He would make them a great nation and give that nation land as an inheritance (32:11–13).

God in His mercy relented of His decision to destroy Israel (32:14).

He changed His course of action but not His character. He remained holy and just.

Moses' Execution of Justice

Moses headed down the mountain with the Ten Commandments in his hands (32:15, 16). Joshua joined him along the way. Joshua thought the noise coming from Israel's camp was the sound of war (32:17). Moses told Joshua the sound was singing. The volume was indicative of the Israelites' reckless abandon in worshiping their god.

When Moses arrived on the scene, he threw down the tablets in righteous anger. The broken tablets served to illustrate that Israel had broken God's commands. Moses then took the idol, burned it, grounded it into powder, scattered it on the water, and made the Israelites drink it.

11. Read Exodus 32:20. Why would Moses make the Israelites drink the remnants of their idol?

Perhaps even Aaron had to drink the idol-ridden water, for Moses asked Aaron why *he* had brought such great sin on the people (32:21).

Sensing his responsibility as Israel's leader in Moses' absence, Aaron first blamed the people for being set on evil. Aaron then made up a tale about the idol making itself (32:22–24).

12. Why wouldn't Aaron admit his guilt? What would motivate him to lie?

Aaron did what was convenient for himself when the Israelites asked for an idol. He let them have their way, failing to provide any restraint (32:25). But he turned on them after Moses came back to camp, taking none of the blame himself.

13. How would you describe Aaron's actions in helping the people commit idolatry and then covering it up?

Moses stood at the entrance of the camp and asked those who were
on the Lord's side to come to him. The sons of Levi did so. Moses had
them go through the camp to kill their fellow Israelites who were still
persisting in idolatrous worship. Three thousand died as a result (32:26–
28). The Levites were set apart for the Lord when they returned to Moses.
Later God would appoint the Levites to be in charge of the tabernacle and
all of its furnishings (cf. Num. 1:50–53).

Moses' Second Appeal to God's Mercy

The people had repented, but their sin needed to be atoned for.
Moses told the people he was going to go to God to see if he could make
atonement for their sin (Exod. 32:30). Moses returned to God and asked
Him to forgive Israel's sin. If God was unwilling, then he asked that God
would blot his name out of God's *book* (32:31, 32). Moses was offering
himself as the ransom for Israel so they would not need to experience
God's judgment. The *book* was perhaps God's record of those who had
inherited eternal life (cf. Dan. 12:1). More likely it was the book that recorded the census, meaning Moses was willing to die on behalf of Israel.
Either way, Moses was quite sincere in his desire to see Israel forgiven.

14. Read Deuteronomy 9:18, 19. What did Moses do on behalf of
    Israel?

God did not take Moses up on his offer to be the ransom for those
who had sinned (Exod. 32:33). Moses could not stand in their place. God
had to discipline Israel. He later sent a plague as part of the punishment
for their idolatry (32:34, 35).

In addition, God said He would no longer lead Israel. Instead, an
angel would go in His place (33:1, 2). God said He could not go with Israel
because He would destroy them for being a stiff-necked people if He was
with them (33:3). The people mourned when they heard God's decision
(33:4–6).

God's relationship with Israel had changed. Moses moved his tent far
outside the camp and met with God there (33:7). The separation between
God and the people was a result of their sin. God's presence at Moses' tent

was signified by the cloud. When the people saw God's presence with Moses, they stood in the doorways of their tents and worshiped God (33:8–11).

Understandably, Moses was nervous about God's decision not to go before Israel as they went to the Promised Land. Moses appealed to God's grace and asked God to consider that the Israelites were *His* people. God responded by saying His presence would go with Moses (33:12–14).

Moses went on to say that God's presence was what made Israel different from the rest of the nations. God again responded by saying He would go with Israel (33:15–17). Israel didn't deserve God's presence, but God would go with them because He is gracious.

God's Self-revelation

God's glory includes all He is: His justice in punishing Israel, His mercy in not destroying them, and His grace in agreeing to go with them to the Promised Land. Moses wanted to see God's glory manifested before him (33:18). But that would not be possible, for no one can see God's fullness and live (33:20). So God agreed to reveal some of His glory to Moses. He told Moses He would hide him with His hand while He passed by. When He removed His hand, Moses would see the afterglow of His glory (33:21–23).

15. Why would it be important for Moses to catch a glimpse of God's glory?

That God forgave Israel is evident in chapter 34. God had Moses make another set of tablets on which He would write the Ten Commandments. When God descended on Sinai to write the Ten Commandments, He passed by Moses as He had promised and revealed His name (34:5). God's *name* is essentially synonymous with His *glory*.

16. Read Exodus 34:5–7. What did God reveal about Himself?

Israel's idolatry gave God an opportunity to reveal His glorious name. In response to God's glory, Moses bowed his head and worshiped (34:8).

Moses then petitioned God, asking Him once again to go among the people, to pardon their iniquity, and to take the people as His inheritance (34:9).

God demonstrated His glory by renewing His covenant with Israel. He reiterated to Moses the stipulations of the covenant and inscribed the Ten Commandments on new tablets (34:10–28).

Israel deserved to be wiped out because of their idolatry. They did experience repercussions from their sin as a result of God's justice, but God in His mercy didn't utterly destroy them. And by His grace He agreed to lead them.

MAKING IT PERSONAL

God's justice, mercy, and grace were evident when God sent His Son to die on the cross for our sins. Christ's death satisfied God's justice so He might withhold punishment for our sins by His mercy and provide eternal life by His grace.

17. How have you responded to God's glory?

18. How should you respond to God's glory?

Every day you experience God's glory, especially His grace. God's grace comforts you when you have pain, strengthens you for the tasks He calls us to, and provides the power to overcome sin in your life.

19. How has God's grace been seen in your life recently?

20. For what pain, task, or sin might you need to ask God to show you His glorious grace?

I AM
Atoner

▶ ## Scripture Focus

Exod. 35–40; Lev. 1—27

Theme

God is holy and provides for both our positional and our practical holiness.

Memory Verse

"Speak unto all the congregation of the children of Israel, and say unto them, Ye shall be holy: for I the LORD your God am holy"
(Leviticus 19:2).

GETTING STARTED

Most daily tasks are so mundane that we do them almost robotically. Showering, shaving, getting dressed, loading the dishwasher, emptying the dishwasher, paying bills, buying groceries, unloading groceries, putting away groceries, sweeping the floor, driving to work, driving home from work. Just think of all the free time we would have if we could do a mundane task just once and never have to do it again.

1. What daily task do you wish you could do just one more time and never have to do again?

2. How would you respond to having to make sacrifices every day, being repeatedly covered in animal blood and guts?

The sacrifices that priests were to make to atone for Israel's sin are detailed in the book of Leviticus. The sacrifices continued year after year. Christ's death on the cross was also for atonement of sin, but it was a once-for-all atonement. This study will examine the tabernacle, priesthood, and sacrifices that God put in place to provide atonement for Israel's sin.

God's Place of Worship

After Israel's sin in making an idol, God gave the people an opportunity to give materials for the tabernacle's construction voluntarily (Exod. 35:5, 29). As a result, more than enough was given to provide for the construction of the tabernacle (36:5–7).

God also provided artisans to make the tabernacle furniture and the many pieces, fabrics, and coverings for the construction of the tabernacle. The artisans were specially equipped by God (36:2). They were led by Bezalel, who personally oversaw the making of each piece of furniture for the tabernacle (35:30–35). All of the work was done just as God had commanded (39:43).

Moses then oversaw the putting together of the tabernacle on the first day of the first month of the second year (40:17).

3. Read Exodus 40:19–32. What phrase in these verses describes how the tabernacle was put together and furnished?

Moses involvement in the construction of the tabernacle showed the people that they were to serve God and take His commands seriously. They weren't Moses' people; they were God's people. Moses' attention to detail was recorded in the Bible as a testimony to God's right to determine what Israel should believe and practice (cf. Exod. 25:40; Heb. 8:4, 5).

4. Read Exodus 25:40; Hebrews 8:4, 5. How should God's expectations concerning His instructions help to shape our approach to His Word in general?

5. Read Exodus 40:34. What indicated God's approval of how the tabernacle was constructed?

When the tabernacle was complete, the glory of the Lord filled the tabernacle. Apparently God revealed His glory to the point that no one could enter the tabernacle (40:35). What kept them out was God's absolute holiness. God is totally set apart from sin. The picture of God alone in His tabernacle sets up the book of Leviticus. Leviticus presents God as the holy *Atoner* of sin. God provided atonement for sin based on unblemished sacrifices and then expected Israel to live up to His standard of holiness.

God's Atoning Sacrifices

Once the tabernacle was in place, God communicated the various laws that would govern Israel's worship of Him through the Levites' priestly service. The book of Leviticus is predominantly about that service.

Leviticus starts with a description of each of the five sacrifices the priests were to administer on behalf of the people: the burnt, grain, peace, sin, and trespass offerings (Lev. 1–7). God required all animal sacrifices to be without blemish (1:3; 3:1; 4:3; 5:15), meaning they were to have nothing obviously wrong with them. And grain was to be offered without leaven, which was a symbol of sin (2:11). No animal is perfect, but those chosen for sacrifices were to at least have the appearance of perfection. Atoning sacrifices had to be *without blemish* to be accepted by God. Eventually Christ would come as the final, perfect sacrifice for the atonement of sins. The animals sacrificed in the Old Testament were merely a shadow of His final, once-for-all sacrifice (Heb. 10:1–10).

6. Read Hebrews 10:1. What could the animal sacrifices never accomplish?

The without-blemish requirement also showed that the innocent was dying on behalf of the guilty. The undeserving animal was the recipient of the deserving person's punishment. The death of the innocent for the guilty again pictured Christ's death for the guilty sinner (Rom. 5:6–11).

Atonement for sin always requires bloodshed (Lev. 17:11; Heb. 9:22). The person bringing the sacrifice would lay his hand on the animal's head and lean heavily on it to identify with the animal (Lev. 1:4). The animal's blood was then shed in the place of the person bringing the sacrifice. The animal's shed blood *atoned for* the person's sin. However, committing more sins brought the need for more sacrifices. There was no once-for-all sacrifice for sin in the tabernacle system.

7. How does the connection between sin and shed blood affect your understanding of the seriousness of sin?

Along with the five daily sacrifices were the yearly sacrifices made by the high priest (Lev. 16). On the Day of Atonement the high priest was to go to the tabernacle with a bullock and a ram, which he sacrificed for his sins and those of his family (16:6, 11). The priest also brought two goats and a ram, which he used on behalf of the people. He put off his normal priestly clothing, with its colors and embroidery and fringes, and put on robes of plain white linen (16:4). The high priest alone carried out the ritual; no one helped him (16:17). He went into the Holy of Holies only on this one day of the year, but he went in twice: once for himself and once for the people.

The two goats constituted one offering. The first was sacrificed as a sin offering (16:15). The priest confessed the sins of the nation on the head of the second goat, which was taken into a *land not inhabited* from which the animal could not return (16:20–22). The sacrifice on the Day of Atonement had to happen every year (16:34).

It is important to remember that the atoning sacrifices were not offered to secure the Israelites' salvation. Their salvation came through their faith in God. Salvation has always been by grace through faith. Israel's atoning sacrifices served to cover their sins and thereby restore their fellowship with God. Believers today don't need to offer sacrifices to take care of their daily sin. When we as believers sin, we confess our sins directly to God, and He is faithful to forgive our sins based on Christ's death on the cross (1 John 1:9).

Christ's death on the cross is the basis of our salvation. Christ paid the penalty for our sin once and for all. We accept His payment for our sins by faith (Rom. 5:1; Eph. 2:8, 9).

God's Consecrated Priesthood

Once the offerings were detailed, it was time for the consecration, or setting apart, of the priesthood. Moses gathered the congregation of the people before him and did as the Lord commanded. He washed Aaron and his sons (including Nadab and Abihu), anointed them with oil to set them apart for their priestly service, and clothed them in their priestly garments (Lev. 8:1–13). Aaron and his sons then made an offering for themselves (Heb. 7:27) before making offerings to set apart the altar (Exod. 8:14–17). They continued the process by offering a ram as a burnt offering of worship and consecration (Lev. 8:18–21). The final offering was another ram offered to install the priests in their offices (8:22–29). Moses applied blood from the second ram to the priests' right ears, right thumbs, and right great toes (8:23, 24). Most likely this application of the blood symbolized the consecration of the priests to hear God, do His will, and walk in His ways. The priests were to give their lives to total obedience and service to the Lord.

The consecration of the priests continued for the next week. God demanded Aaron and his sons stay at the door of the tabernacle night and day for an entire week as part of their preparation to become priests (8:35). God was communicating to the priests and all of Israel the importance of being set apart for His service.

8. Read Leviticus 8:35. How important was it for the priests to obey God's instructions?

9. Read Leviticus 8:36. How carefully did Aaron and his sons obey God's will?

After the week was up, the priests conducted their first day of service before the Lord on behalf of the people of Israel (9:1–22). The final official event of the first day of the priests' service included a miraculous display of God's presence.

10. Read Leviticus 9:23, 24. If you were an Israelite watching the event, how do you think you would have responded to God's miraculous display of His presence?

The priests had been obedient in their consecration ceremonies, and the Lord showed His presence on the first day of service in the tabernacle. All was going well until two priests decided to do things their way.

God's Demand for Holiness

Nadab and Abihu, Aaron's two oldest sons, were fully aware of the importance of being set apart to God. They took part in the consecration procedures, and they had just spent a week of consecration in the tabernacle. They would be without excuse if they chose to deviate from God's laws regarding the sacrificial system and priesthood. Yet they offered incense to the Lord with strange, profane fire, meaning their incense offering was not acceptable to God (10:1).

11. Why do you think Nadab and Abihu offered profane fire to God?

Nadab and Abihu violated God's holiness by their disobedience. They did not live separated unto the Lord. They lived according to their own rules, taking their service to God as priests either lightly or carelessly. Either way, they failed to take God's holiness seriously.

After Nadab and Abihu disobeyed God's clear commands about offering incense to Him, God devoured them with fire (10:2).

12. Read Leviticus 10:2. Do you think God's slaying of Aaron's sons was fair? Explain.

13. Who were Nadab and Abihu really serving when they offered their
    incense?

God is never pleased when we disobey His clear will in an attempt to
please Him. He wants us to have a deep appreciation and respect for His
holiness.

The Israelites watched as Aaron's cousins carried the bodies of Nadab
and Abihu through the camp (10:4, 5). No doubt those who actually saw
the bodies stood in stunned silence.

14. How would such a scene have affected Israel's understanding of
    worship?

God didn't always act with such dramatic and quick judgment on His
people, but this event was important in Israel's history. Israel was beginning the official priestly service, and God needed to show His people that
His law was not up for personal interpretation.

Moses told Aaron and his remaining sons neither to mourn for Nadab
and Abihu nor to leave the tabernacle (10:6, 7). A priest's role was to
worship God and not to mourn. The priests were God's representatives
before the people. For them to mourn publically would have been a con-
tradiction in the eyes of the people. God permitted Aaron and his family
to mourn inwardly and privately.

In case Aaron missed the importance of what had just happened, God
spoke directly to him (10:8, 9). He told him to refrain from mixing strong
drink with tabernacle service lest he die. The reason for this was twofold:
to keep a distinction between what was holy and what was unholy and to
teach the Children of Israel all of God's statutes. God wanted Aaron to understand fully the importance of respecting Him while worshiping Him.

Moses understood the need for the priests to be careful to respect God
by obeying His instructions for the various sacrifices. When he made a
careful inquiry into what Eleazar and Ithamar, Aaron's sons, were doing,
he spotted an inconsistency (10:16–18). Aaron gave an explanation for the

inconsistency to Moses' satisfaction (10:19, 20).

God atoned for Israel's sin, but the atoning sacrifices had to be conducted according to His instructions. God is holy. Israel had to treat Him as such.

God's Laws for Holy Living and Worship

The rest of the book of Leviticus gives God's laws for holy living and holy worship (11–16). While this section of the book doesn't provide many devotional thoughts, it does help to communicate God's demands for pure and holy living.

The next section of Leviticus (17–22) concerns more holy living laws about topics such as slaughtering beasts and sexual morality. Chapters 23–25 provide for additional laws concerning the feasts, the care of the tabernacle, blasphemy, the Sabbath year, and the year of jubilee. The section on blasphemy (24:10–16) includes an illustration of a man who blasphemed God. The man was stoned according to God's direction (24:13–16). What a vivid illustration of the need for God's young nation to honor God's holy name.

15. Read Leviticus 19:2. Why were the Israelites to be holy?

God came to dwell with Israel. But for them to maintain fellowship with Him, they needed to live holy lives (26:3, 11, 12). The last main section of Leviticus spells that out clearly (26). Israel would enjoy prosperity and safety in the Promised Land as they managed their lives according to God's law (26:3–13). But they would experience disease, famine, attacks by wild beasts, and captivity for failing to manage their lives according to God's law (26:14–39). However, God would honor His covenant with them if they confessed their iniquity and humbled their uncircumcised, or disloyal, hearts (26:40–45).

The tabernacle, the priesthood, the sacrifices, and the laws for holy living were designed by God to guide Israel as they managed their lives with Him in their presence. He provided for their atonement of sin, but they needed to live according to His directives to be pleasing to Him. Unfortunately Israel wandered often from the Lord. The next chapter in

Israel's history is replete with doubt and fears instead of belief and faith.

God has cleansed us from our sins and has declared us righteous. But that does not give us a license to do whatever we want. He expects us to live holy lives separated unto Him (1 Pet. 1:13–19). God dwells in us in the Person of the Holy Spirit. And He gives us the power and grace to live pleasing to God.

16. How has learning about Israel's interaction with God in the tabernacle setting helped you appreciate God's presence in you?

17. Is your life characterized by holy living? Are you growing spiritually? Allow God's presence to make a spiritual difference in your life.

18. You can enter boldly to God's throne of grace at any moment. What might keep you from taking advantage of immediate access to God's throne?

19. God longs to commune with you. What will you do to make time to commune with Him every day?

I AM
Gracious Giver

▶ Scripture Focus

Num. 1—14

Theme

God is a gracious giver of blessings, and He is for believers.

Memory Verse

"What shall we then say to these things? If God be for us, who can be against us? He that spared not his own Son, but delivered him up for us all, how shall he not with him also freely give us all things?" (Romans 8:31, 32).

GETTING STARTED

Vacations provide a time to get away from the normal routines and responsibilities. Unfortunately traveling to the vacation destination can be so stressful that it offsets the positives gained from the vacation.

1. Describe a bad experience you had traveling to and from a vacation destination. How did the travelers respond?

2. How did the anticipation of the destination help alleviate some of the anxiety caused by the bad circumstances?

The Israelites expected the journey to the Promised Land to be as good as the destination. They complained when it wasn't. God's response to them helps us see Him as the gracious giver.

God Provided for Israel

Numbers is not written chronologically. Number 1—6 happened after the events in 7:1—10:10. This study takes a chronological approach, picking up Israel's journey to the Promised Land at their departure from Mount Sinai (7). The nation gave offerings to the Lord to support the worship of God. They had a priesthood in place (8:5–26) and a brand new tabernacle as God's dwelling place. They celebrated their second Passover as a freed nation (9:1–14) and enjoyed God's presence (9:15–23). God even instituted a communication system using two silver trumpets (10:1–10). The various signals would tell each tribe when it was time for them to move out so the nation's departures were orderly. Moses also used the trumpets to assemble Israel.

3. Read Numbers 10:9. What purpose would the trumpets serve in the Promised Land?

4. Read Numbers 10:10. What do God's instructions in this verse assume about Israel's future?

Before moving out, God had Moses complete a census (1). The emphasis was on numbering the men who could go to war (1:46). God then provided instructions on how the tribes were to be arranged around the tabernacle (2). God's dwelling place was the hub of the camp, with the priests from the tribe of Levi dwelling between the people and the tabernacle. Moses numbered the Levites and detailed the responsibilities for each major division of Levites (3; 4). Moses ended Israel's stay at Sinai with additional instructions (5:1—6:21).

The benediction God gave to Moses to give to Aaron and the Levites is rich with meaning and emotion (6:22–27). That it is written as poetry means it was to illicit a deep response from Israel. The prayer serves to reveal God's desire to bless Israel (6:27). His intentions for Israel were always for their good, beginning with His promises to the patriarchs. The words *and keep thee* point to God's desire to preserve Israel so that they might enjoy

His blessings into the future, particularly in the Promised Land.

The Lord's face shining on the Israelites is a reference to the Lord's presence with Israel (6:28). Moses' face shone after he was in God's presence (Exod. 34:29–35). God's presence would bring Israel grace, favors they wouldn't deserve but that God delighted in providing for them.

The last section of the prayer is climatic (Num. 6:26). It called for the Lord to turn His face toward Israel and to give them peace. *Peace* communicates a sense of completeness and wellness of soul as a result of God's attention. *Lift up his countenance upon thee* is the equivalent of God smiling at Israel. God delighted in giving Israel His gracious gifts. As the priests prayed this benediction that the Lord prescribed, the Lord would identify Himself with His people and bless them (6:27).

5.   Read Numbers 6:22–27. What three words would you use to describe God's intentions for Israel?

God's desire for Israel was to recognize Him as their giver of blessings. He desired for them to be *content* and *rejoicing*, especially as they looked ahead to the wonderful blessings of the Promised Land. Israel disappointed almost immediately.

Israel Complained

Reading Numbers chronologically helps show the stark contrast between the Lord's desires to bless Israel in the priestly benediction (6:22–27) and Israel's immediate rebellion against Him as they left Sinai (11:1–3).

The people complained on just the third day of their journey (11:1). Why Israel complained is not as important as knowing it displeased God. Remember that complaining is expressing one's dissatisfaction with God.

In His displeasure, God sent a fire to the outskirts of Israel's camp to burn up some of the Israelites. The people cried out to Moses who then prayed to God (11:2). God quenched the fire and spared Israel any more harm. The place was called *Taberah*, meaning *burning* (11:3).

We can surmise that Israel was dissatisfied with their circumstances. No doubt they could imagine being in better circumstances or in a better place. In other words, God had chosen not to provide them with the very best circumstances they could imagine.

6. Why do you suppose God didn't provide the very best for Israel while they were in the wilderness?

The wilderness was not Israel's final destination. God didn't promise them a *wilderness* flowing with milk and honey. That blessing was for the Promised Land that awaited them at the end of their journey.

Israel Craved Meat

As was often the case with Israel, they had a short memory when it came to God's discipline of them. Their next round of complaining was apparently led by foreigners, possibly Egyptians, who had left Egypt with them (11:4). The mixed multitude among the Israelites craved meat. They drew Israel to join them in their complaining. Israel questioned, *Who shall give us flesh to eat?* They then romanticized what life was like for them in Egypt: eating fish *freely* (11:5). The Egyptians probably did allow Israel to eat the fish readily found in the rivers and waterways of Egypt. But the Egyptians didn't make for good masters otherwise. How offensive to God for Israel to think that Egypt was a better place to be than in the wilderness with Him.

7. Who was ultimately responsible for providing Israel with fish and vegetables to eat in Egypt?

Israel overstated their current situation, saying their whole being was *dried away* because they had nothing but *manna* before their eyes (11:6–10). The manna provided for their nutrition and kept them alive in an otherwise unforgiving wilderness.

Moses quickly grew weary of the people's complaining. He took his weariness to God and asked why he was responsible for a people he had not conceived (11:11, 12). He asked God where he could possibly find meat for all the people (11:13). Overwhelmed by the task of caring for two million people, Moses asked God to just take his life if that was the way God was going to treat him (11:14, 15). Obviously Moses had a troubled heart. The task *was* too much for him to bear.

God responded to Moses and the people. For Moses he appointed seventy men on whom He would bring His Spirit so that they could help Moses (11:16, 17). Perhaps the unspoken rebuke for Moses was that he could have had help had he simply asked.

In response to Israel God said He would give Israel meat to eat, but He would use it to judge them (11:18).

8. Read Numbers 11:19, 20. Why was Israel's complaining so serious?

Israel would eat so much meat that it would start coming out of their nostrils. The picture is of them gorging themselves on the meat, trying to find satisfaction from it.

9. Why would Israel not find satisfaction in eating the meat?

Israel already had all they needed to find peace and satisfaction in their present situation. Manna was God's gracious provision for their needs. But they looked at what manna was not and concluded that God was not the giver of good blessings. Instead they believed He was responsible for keeping them from their ultimate fulfillment. They concluded that God was holding out on them and therefore wasn't worth having around. They despised God's presence and longed to be out from under His leadership.

Moses interrupted God's judgment with some doubts of his own (11:21, 22). He questioned where God was going to come up with such a tremendous amount of meat to feed around two million people. But God asked Moses, *Is the Lord's hand waxed short?* (11:23). God said Moses would witness His ability to do as He desires, thereby rebuking Moses' lack of faith.

Moses left to tell the people God's word. As God promised, His Spirit came on the elders who had gathered around the tabernacle (11:24–30).

Also as God had said, He sent quail around Israel's camp in each direction. The people, believing the meat would bring them contentment stayed up all night collecting the birds (11:31, 32). But before they even had a chance to chew their first bite, God struck them with a plague, killing some while the meat was still in their mouths (11:33).

10. Read 1 Timothy 6:6. What would Israel have gained by being content with manna?

Israel moved on to Hazeroth. No doubt they wanted to leave the *graves of craving* behind (11:34). But Hazeroth would bring its own problems.

Miriam and Aaron Criticized Moses

The next crisis was one of jealousy. Miriam and Aaron criticized Moses' selection of a wife (12:1). They spoke against him because he had married an Ethiopian (Cushite). But their problem with Moses actually had nothing to do with his marriage. Their real problem was with his special relationship with the Lord (12:2). God dealt with the real issue. He called Moses, Miriam, and Aaron to appear before Him at the tabernacle (12:4).

11. What did Miriam and Aaron conclude about God by criticizing His choice of Moses as the leader of His people?

Remember that Aaron had failed miserably when God left him in charge of the people when Moses was on Mount Sinai (Exod. 32).

12. How do you think Aaron would have done at leading God's people based on his failed attempt?

God spoke face-to-face with Moses, revealing some of His glory and allowing Moses to see His *similitude* (12:6–8). So God asked Miriam and Aaron why they would dare to speak against Moses. Having His anger aroused, God departed. Miriam subsequently became leprous. Aaron pleaded with Moses and Moses prayed for Miriam. God would heal her, but only after she spent a week as a leper outside the camp. The rest of the congregation waited for Miriam to be restored before moving on.

Again, discontentment with God was the root of this problem. Miriam in particular was not content with how God had used her. She had been instrumental in preserving Moses' life and had taken part in the song written to praise God for deliverance from Egypt. Yet much like the Israelites who desired meat, she believed God was not a giver of good blessings but rather a robber of her ultimate fulfillment. She wanted to be more than God had called her to be.

Israel Rejected God

The belief that God was not a giver of good blessings spread to the nation after they arrived at the doorstep of the Promised Land in Kadesh Barnea. Moses commanded the people to go up and possess the land (cf. Deut. 1:21). The people asked him to send spies in the land first (1:22). Moses agreed with their request, and God graciously allowed it (Num. 13:1, 2). Moses appointed a man from each tribe, including Joshua and Caleb, to be the spies (13:3–16). The spies were to report on both the land and the people (13:17–20).

The spies' first stop in the Promised Land was Hebron (13:21, 22). They noticed that the descendants of Anak lived there. The descendants of Anak were giants according to the spies' report.

13. Read Numbers 13:22; Genesis 23:1, 2; 25:7–10; 35:27–29; 50:13, 14. What should the spies have noted about the city of Hebron?

Hebron should have bolstered the spies' faith; instead it made them afraid. They focused on the obstacles, not on God's promises.

The only other place the spies noted in particular was the valley of Eshcol, named for its enormous clusters of grapes. The spies took a cluster and carried it on a pole between two men because it was so big (13:23, 24).

After forty days in the land, the spies returned with their report. They confirmed that the land indeed flowed with milk and honey, meaning it was a bountiful land that brought forth much fruit. They showed the giant grapes they had carried back, along with pomegranates and figs (13:25–27).

14. How should the people have reacted to the bountiful land report?

The spies also talked about the big cities and the big people (13:28, 29).

Ten of the spies said they were not able to overcome them. Their report must have caused a discouraging response, for Caleb had to quiet the people. He said they would be able to overcome the people in the land. He encouraged them to go forward (13:30). But the other spies insisted *they are stronger than we* (13:31–33). Yet the bountiful Promised Land was God's gracious gift.

15. Read Numbers 14:1–4. What did the Israelites conclude about God?

The people complained and decided to go back to Egypt instead of into the Promised Land.

16. Read Numbers 14:5–9. What did Joshua and Caleb believe about God?

God presented Israel with the very best He had ever offered them. They flat out rejected His blessing and Him. They never really believed God was for them (14:10). They never trusted His goodness. They were certain that God's idea to bring them out of Egypt would turn out bad in the end. And so in the end it did for the naysayers and complainers. They never entered the Promised Land but died in the barren wilderness (14:29), a sad testimony of missed blessings because of mistrust in God (14:11). The children they claimed to protect would inherit the land without them forty years later (14:31).

MAKING IT PERSONAL

17. How do you know God is not against you? (See Romans 8:31–39.)

18. Have you been content with your lot in life? Explain.

19. What reasons do you have to rejoice in the Lord with thanksgiving?

I AM
Powerful Proclaimer

▶ Scripture Focus

Num. 14:39—24:25

Theme

God's power could never be overcome by another.

> **Memory Verse**
>
> *"God is not a man, that he should lie; neither the son of man, that he should repent: hath he said, and shall he not do it? or hath he spoken, and shall he not make it good?" (Numbers 23:19).*

GETTING STARTED

Some dogs have learned to mimic their owner's words. When an owner hears her dog say *I love you*, she may feel like the dog is actually communicating to her. But reality is, the dog is just doing a trick to get a treat. *I love you* is the same as *blah blah blah* to a dog.

1. If your pet could talk, what do you think it would want to say to you?

2. How do you think you would react if your pet talked to you?

This study introduces the character of Balaam, an ancient diviner. God used Balaam's donkey to get Balaam's attention. Balaam learned that God could never be overpowered or outsmarted.

Israel's Rebellions

God condemned Israel to spend forty years in the wilderness when they chose to reject Him and the Promised Land. So every Israelite twenty years old and older would die during the forty years of wilderness wandering (Num. 14:33, 34). The people tried to change God's decision by invading the Promised Land after He handed down His death sentence (14:39–45).

3. Read Numbers 14:39–45. What did the people learn about their ability to overcome God's will?

God's ban on the Promised Land would not be forever. And when it came time for the Israelites to enter the land, no one would be able to keep them out. That is why God continued to give Moses instructions about Israel's worship of Him in the land that He was giving to them (15:1–21). God also gave them additional laws concerning unintentional sins and presumptuous sins.

God then instructed them on the punishment for breaking the Sabbath. Some in the congregation found a man collecting sticks on the Sabbath. The people stoned the man according to God's command (15:32–36). Obviously the Israelites were to take God's commands seriously. So God gave them a way to remember their need to obey Him.

4. Read Numbers 15:37–41. Why did the Israelites need a reminder to obey God?

The events recorded after God's instructions concerning the tassels (*fringes*) proved why Israel needed them. Korah, a Levite, led a rebellion of Reubenites and other men of reputation, accusing Moses and Aaron of exalting themselves above the rest of the people and criticizing Moses specifically for acting like a prince over them (16:3, 13). No doubt Korah's ambition was to garner enough support to overthrow both Moses and Aaron. Since his generation was already condemned to die in the wilderness, perhaps he and his rebels thought they could change the curse if they got rid of their leaders. They blamed Moses, both for taking them from Egypt, a land they considered flowing with milk and honey, and for failing to bring them into the land (16:12–14).

God judged Korah and his two fellow rebels by opening the earth to swallow them up (16:31–33). The rest of the *respectable* men that questioned Moses were struck by God's fire (16:34, 35). The judgment was a sign to the rest of Israel that Moses was a leader by the will of God; he was not a self-appointed leader (16:28). This crisis proved again that God's will cannot be thwarted.

The people failed to learn the lesson. They blamed Moses and Aaron for killing the people (16:41). God plagued them until Aaron mercifully intervened (16:42–50). God then proved that Aaron was His choice to be priest. His rod produced blossoms and brought forth almonds, while the rods of all the other tribes remained dead (17:1–11). God's will could not be overcome.

Moses' Rebellion

The record of Israel's time in the wilderness is sparse. But what is recorded is important, and no event is greater than Moses' rebellion at Kadesh. The nation was most likely nearing the end of their wilderness time when they complained again about not having water. Once again God told Moses the water would come from a rock. Moses was to speak to it, but he hit it twice with his rod instead (20:8–11). The water came forth, but God was not happy. Because Moses and Aaron had not hallowed God before the congregation, God would not allow Moses and Aaron to enter the Promised Land (20:12).

Moses failed to believe God in some manner. Calling the people *rebels* and asking them about needing to *fetch* water from the rock are perhaps clues that Moses was frustrated that God was going to provide water for the people without disciplining them in some way. Whatever the reason, hitting the rock in anger instead of speaking to it was a rebellious act against God.

5. Read Numbers 20:12. What message did Moses send to the people about submitting to God's will?

After the nation journeyed from Kadesh to Mount Hor (20:22), Aaron died on the mountain according to God's will (20:22–29). Israel then defeated the Canaanites at Hormah before the journey got laborious (21:1–4). They complained about what God had been giving them, manna, and about not having water. This time God did judge them. He sent deadly snakes (21:5, 6). Moses erected a bronze serpent to which those who were bitten could look for salvation (21:7–9). Perhaps the judgment and the salvation were a lesson for Moses: he could trust God to be just, merciful, and gracious—all part of God's glory God had revealed to Moses on Mount Sinai (cf. Exod. 33:17–19).

Balaam's Futility

While Israel continued on, a new character entered the narrative. Balaam was a notable diviner familiar to multiple ancient people groups. He used animal entrails and nature to determine a god's will. He also cursed and blessed people to try to influence the gods. God's message through the account of Balaam is clear: no one can ever overpower or outsmart God.

6. Read Numbers 22:1–4. What was Balak's disposition toward Israel?

7. Read Deuteronomy 2:8, 9. Did Balak need to fear Israel?

8. Read Numbers 22:5, 6. How confident was Balak in Balaam's ability to influence the course of history?

Balak's words about Balaam's blessings and curses are similar to God's words to Abram in Genesis 12:3.

9. Read Genesis 12:3. What did God say would happen to those who cursed Abram?

Even if Balaam did curse Israel, he would in essence be cursing himself.

Balak sent two entourages to Balaam, attempting to convince him to accept the job of cursing Israel. But God met with Balaam before he responded to each request. God instructed Balaam to deny the first request. However, God allowed Balaam to accept the second request with the caveat to do only what God said (Num. 22:20). Many commentators view Balaam's words during these negotiations as ploys for a larger payment.

Nevertheless, Balaam rose early *and went with the princes of* Moab (22:21). God's response to Balaam's actions is surprising (22:22). The best explanation is to allow other passages to aid our understanding. Both 2 Peter 2:15 and Jude 11 criticize Balaam for gaining from wrongdoing. Evidently Balaam was motivated more by a desire for the riches promised by Balak than by a desire to do what God wanted. Although Balaam had met with God in some fashion, he apparently believed he could override God's will and gain financially.

The account of Balaam and his donkey is one of the most comical pictures in the Bible. Three times the Angel of the Lord stood in front of the donkey, causing it to stop (22:23–26). The third time Balaam hit the donkey. It responded to let Balaam know it wasn't trying to be rebellious. The Lord opened Balaam's eyes so he, too, could see the Angel of the Lord (22:27–31). The Angel of the Lord said he had come to stop Balaam because his way was perverse. Balaam confessed his sin and offered to turn back (22:32–34).

10. Read Numbers 22:35. What did the Angel of the Lord tell Balaam?

Balaam was a learned, proud man. God used the speech of a donkey to teach Balaam just how insignificant he was. The humor we appreciate in this story is representative of the ridiculousness of someone believing he can override or control God.

Balaam's Oracles

When the diviner met the king, Balak asked Balaam to curse Israel; however, Balaam, constrained by God, *blessed* Israel. This cycle repeated three times. Prior to the first two oracles of blessing, Balaam performed a pagan sacrificial ritual. God still used Balaam in a significant way. Balaam's oracles blessed Israel and prophesied of the Messiah.

Balaam's first blessing (23:7–10) is connected with God's covenantal promises made to the patriarchs (Gen. 12:1–3; 26:1–5; 35:9–15). The blessing recognized that even if Balaam were to utter words of cursing, he could not change God's favorable disposition toward Israel. The blessing was especially concerned with the promises that Israel would be a great nation.

Balaam's rhetorical question regarding Israel's population (Num. 23:10) parallels God's promise to make Israel as numerous as the stars in the sky and the sand on the seashore. Balaam even added that he wished he could be part of Israel and take part in their blessing.

11. Read Numbers 23:11, 12. How did Balaam respond to Balak?

Balaam's actions throughout this extended text do not indicate that he became a genuine believer. But for moments at least, Balaam understood that God could not be overpowered or outsmarted.

Balaam began his second oracle focusing Balak's attention on God's immutability (23:18, 19). God does not change. God promised Abraham and his descendants a land, seed, and blessing, and God could never renege on those promises. God is always faithful.

This oracle focused on Israel's great strength. Numbers 23:22 compares Israel to a *unicorn*, or strong wild ox.

12. Read Numbers 23:3. What did the oracle say about the power of sorcery and divination in relation to Israel?

God had already blessed Israel. There are no loopholes through which God could be overpowered or outsmarted.

13. Read Numbers 23:24. How do you think Balak reacted to the last description of Israel?

Balak's initial response to Balaam's second oracle was to silence

Balaam (23:25). Balak thought that if Balaam could not say anything advantageous for Moab, then he should not say anything at all. Balaam showed the fault in that strategy by saying he must speak the words God had given to him (23:26). He could not overpower God.

At first glance the third oracle appears similar to the second. Many of the same observations made in reference to the second oracle can be applied to the third oracle. A significant difference between the two oracles is found in the pronouns. Balaam's second oracle spoke of *them* in reference to Israel; Balaam's third oracle spoke of *him*. This change in pronouns is significant.

The mysterious references to *him* in 24:3–9 refers to the future Messiah. This understanding is supported by the expansion of the third oracle in 24:15–24. Those verses are about the *latter days* (24:14).

Balak was livid with Balaam (24:10–13). He slapped his hands together for effect and told Balaam to go home without payment. Balaam reiterated that he had to speak what God said even if it meant he would be working for free.

As Balaam departed, he gave a final addendum to the cycle of three oracles. This final poem is the third major poem of the Pentateuch (Gen. 49; Exod. 15) and the second introduced with a focus on the *latter days* (cf. Gen. 49:1).

14. Read Numbers 24:15–24. What descriptors are used for the central person of this oracle?

Balaam's description of an individual Who was coming but not yet near points to the Messiah (Num. 24:17). The further description of Him as a scepter rising out of Israel echoes Genesis 49:10. That verse says the scepter would not depart from Judah. The two poems are obviously referring to the same individual, the promised Messiah.

The reference to the individual as a victorious warrior leader (Num. 24:17–19) closely parallels Genesis 49. Some of the military victories prophesied in this passage happened partly in Old Testament history. Edom, for example, was defeated according to 2 Samuel 8:14; 2 Kings 8:20–22; and Isaiah 63:1–6. However the best explanation for the passage as a whole is to see a future fulfillment of these victories. The names *Edom* and *Seir* could stand for general enemies of God rather than those specific nations.

15. How does comparing Numbers 23:19 to 24:17 affect your faith in God's power?

16. Read Numbers 24:25. What do you think Balak concluded about God after listening to Balaam's oracles?

God's words through Balaam should strengthen our faith in God. He demonstrated that He cannot be overpowered or outsmarted. He communicated that He cannot lie (23:19). That means a lot to us when we consider the prophetic tone of Balaam's last oracle. The Messiah did come, and He is coming again to set up His kingdom on earth. No one or nothing can change God's words. We can put our faith in Him with complete confidence.

MAKING IT PERSONAL

Multiple characters in the passages for this lesson had a run-in with God's powerful will. Each time God proved that His will cannot be overcome. Respect God's power and to seek to *do* rather than *escape* His will.

17. When have you acted as if you didn't need to listen to God?

18. What must you believe about God when you attempt to resist or ignore His will?

Balaam received direct communication from God. Today we have the Bible as His communication to us. We should value the Bible as authoritative in all areas of our lives. The Bible is sufficient instruction for living a godly life.

19. What behaviors evidence that someone values the Bible as authoritative in his life?

20. What will you do this week to increase your respect for God's authoritative Word?

I AM
Loving Lord

▶ **Scripture Focus**

Deut. 1—7:11

Theme

God loves us and desires us to love Him with all our being.

> ### Memory Verses
>
> *"And thou shalt love the LORD thy God with all thine heart, and with all thy soul, and with all thy might. And these words, which I command thee this day, shall be in thine heart"* (Deuteronomy 6:5, 6).

GETTING STARTED

Waiting in line or traffic can drive a person crazy in just a few minutes. Waiting forty years to finally get home is unimaginable. Forty years is a long time to wait for anything.

1. What, if anything, do you remember from forty years ago?

2. How dramatically has your life changed since then?

It had been forty years since Israel left Sinai. The older generation had died off; the new generation needed a renewed message about God and His expectations for them in the Promised Land. Moses' message to them focuses both on God's love for Israel and God's desire for Israel to love Him back.

The book of Deuteronomy is God's preparation of His people for the Promised Land. The book is far more concerned about Israel's heart in response to God than are the books of Leviticus and Numbers. In fact, the word *love* appears more times in Deuteronomy than it does in all other Bible books except for Psalms, Proverbs, Song of Solomon, John, and 1 John. Obviously *love* was an important theme in God's message to His people. He focused on both His love for them and their love for Him.

Since Deuteronomy is a message to God's people, it doesn't move the story of Israel's journey along. Rather, it contains reflections on the past journey, instructions for the present in anticipation of possessing the land, and prophecies about the future. The message was given by God through Moses so the present and future generations might learn to love their loving God.

God's Love for Israel

Moses began his look at Israel's past by recalling what happened when Israel left Mount Sinai (Horeb) for the Promised Land. After the spies had returned from surveying the Promised Land, the people saw the fruit but refused to enter because of the giants in the land.

3. Read Deuteronomy 1:25–28. What did those who refused to enter the land conclude about the Lord?

Moses tried to convince the people to go forward based on God's care for them in the past (1:29–31).

4. Read Deuteronomy 1:29–31. What does the picture of God carrying Israel convey about God's relationship with Israel?

The people refused to believe God. So God judged them; those twenty years and older died at some point over the next forty years (1:32–40).

Deuteronomy 2 briefly recounts the wilderness years and then presents

Israel's second approach to the Promised Land. Interestingly, the main focus in the chapter is on what God did for the Edomites, Moabites, and Ammonites. The Edomites were descendants of Esau (Jacob's brother), and the Moabites and Ammonites were descendants of Lot (Abraham's nephew). God had given an inheritance to both Esau (Gen. 36:6–8; Deut. 2:4, 5) and Lot (Deut. 2:9, 19), so the Israelites were not to attack Edom and Moab as they passed by them.

The Edomites and Moabites both chased giants from their lands. The giants were comparable to those who occupied the Promised Land and had scared the previous generation of Israelites into refusing to enter the land. The record of God's care for Edom, Moab, and Ammon (2:20–22) had to be both an encouragement for Israel as they looked forward and a disappointment as they considered their past. If God provided land for nations because they were simply descended from relatives of the patriarchs, then how much more would He care for the nation He called His own? The former generation of Israelites thought God hated them. They couldn't have been more wrong, as evidenced by God's work on behalf of Edom, Moab, and Ammon and as evidenced by God's care for them during their forty years of wandering (2:7).

Moses then went on to recount the victories over the Kings Sihon and Og, whose territories were east of the Jordan River (2:26—3:11). Moses divided their lands as part of Israel's inheritance (3:12–22). The historical reflection ends with Moses recounting his request to enter the Promised Land. God stood by His decision and told Moses to stop asking. Joshua would lead the people into the Promised Land (3:23–29).

Obeying God's commands and refraining from idolatry would be fundamental to Israel's enjoying their land. God had promised them at Mount Sinai that, if they were obedient and loyal to Him, they would enjoy the land and live long in it (4:9, 10, 23, 40).

5. Deuteronomy 4:23, 24. What caused God to be jealous of Israel's attention?

Israel was more privileged than any other nation (4:32–40). They heard God's voice and received from Him instructions on how to live.

6. Read Deuteronomy 4:37. Why did God choose Abraham to father His nation?

God's relationship with Israel was always based on His love for them. He didn't grow to love them; He loved them with an everlasting love (Jer. 31:3). In the Promised Land He wanted them to love Him back. Loving God made perfect sense for the Israelites after all God had done for them.

Moses reintroduced God's law in the form of the Ten Commandments (Deut. 4:44—6:3). He also included the conversation that had gone on after the giving of the law. God longed for Israel to have hearts that were set on obedience to Him (5:29). His love for Israel was the reason for His longing (7:1–11).

7. Read Deuteronomy 7:1–11. How did God describe His relationship with Israel?

God chose to love Israel. They had nothing that made them better than anyone else (7:7, 8). What a privilege for Israel to know God as loving Lord!

The Extent of Israel's Love for God

After encouraging the people again to be faithful to God, Moses talked about the greatest commandment.

8. Read Deuteronomy 6:4. How does this verse describe God?

9. Why would it be important for the Israelites to understand this description as they approached the Promised Land?

If the content of the law could be summarized in one succinct confessional statement, Deuteronomy 6:4 would likely be that statement. This verse, which later became known to Jews as the *Shema,* communicates several critical concepts. The Hebrew construction of the verse contains no verb after the command to hear. This unusual construction allows four Hebrew words to teach several truths simultaneously. The first truth taught is that God is the LORD. We have learned that LORD is God's covenantal name, a name that focuses on God's faithfulness to His promises. This is the God of the universe. God is not some whimsical, flawed god found in so many ancient religious texts. The true God is faithful; He keeps His word.

Second, this verse teaches the LORD is *our God*. Israel enjoyed a unique and special relationship with God. His relationship with them was not to the exclusion of outsiders but in order to communicate His character to the outsiders.

Third, God is Israel's only God. They were to have no other gods. This truth is why some scholars prefer this phrase to be translated, *The LORD is our God, the LORD alone.* Both the immediate context of chapter 6 and the extended context of Deuteronomy 4:32–40 and 5:7 and 8 shows that this third truth is emphasized in this verse.

> 10. Read Deuteronomy 6:5. What was Israel commanded to do in response to this brief content summary of Israel's faith?

Jesus described the commandment of Deuteronomy 6:5 as the greatest commandment (Matt. 22:37, 38). The natural response to the truth that there is only one God is that His followers should love Him with all their being. The terms *heart, soul,* and *might* in this verse are not precise. The use of these three terms together means to love God with all you are.

> 11. Read Deuteronomy 6:6–9. Where and when were parents to teach their children?

> 12. Share a specific example from your life when you taught children about faith in God using a real life teachable moment.

The command to teach children uses a series of merisms to reinforce the holistic strategy in view. A merism is a rhetorical device that uses a pair of opposites to signify a whole (e.g., *from A to Z* or *from high to low*).

The Israelite parents were to talk about the commands at bedtime, in the morning, and every time in between. As a family and as a community they were to consider the law.

13. What tangible reminders of the Christian faith are in your home?

14. How do you help others, especially children, appreciate the significance of those reminders?

Threats to Israel's Love for God

Unfortunately, there are no guarantees that the redeemed will seek to perpetuate their faith. In fact there are many threats to the faithful transmission of faith. God warned Israel of three threats to passing their faith on to their children.

15. Read Deuteronomy 6:10–12. How would prosperity threaten the transmission of faith once the Israelites entered the rich Promised Land?

Moses challenged the people of Israel before they entered the Promised Land. He warned them about the cities, homes, farms, wells, and material wealth God would give to them as they conquered the land. The nomadic lifestyle they had been living for the past forty years was going to change. God knew this change would tempt Israel to abandon their faith. The new wealth would tempt them to forget that God had delivered them from Egypt. They would be tempted to think they were self-sufficient and that they didn't need God.

16. What are some threats money and possessions pose to today's Christian family?

17. Read Deuteronomy 6:13–15. What gods threatened the perpetuation of Israel's faith?

Jealousy is a sin when manifested in humanity. God, however, is righteously jealous (6:15). He shares His glory with no one. God's jealousy is rooted in His love for Israel.

Pluralism is a belief that multiple beliefs can coexist within the same person or group of people. Israel became pluralistic when they added local deities to their worship. Obviously this practice was intolerable to God.

Pluralism is prevalent in our culture too. People blend Christianity with all sorts of unbiblical beliefs. Pluralism is a serious threat to perpetuating one's faith to the next generation.

18. What are some examples of pluralistic influences on Christianity?

19. Where might people get exposed to these pluralistic forms of Christianity?

Shortly after Israel experienced a spectacular deliverance from Egypt, they sinned against God by doubting He was still with them when they had no water (Exod. 17:7). This incident became a reference point for Israel's repeated episodes of doubt throughout the wilderness wanderings.

Moses challenged Israel not to test God (Deut. 6:16). As Israel conquered the land, temptations to doubt God's presence with them would arise. Doubting God's presence would obviously be a serious threat to establishing their children in their faith in God. Instead of doubting God's presence, the Israelites needed to diligently keep God's commandments (6:17). They needed to be so sure that He was with them that obeying Him became their way of life.

Eventually Israel's doubts about God led to their disobedience and hardship in the land. They never fully realized the blessings God promised them if they would do what was right (6:18), and they were never able to completely conquer the land (6:19). Consequently, future generations were not firmly established in their faith. Doubt of God's presence created an atmosphere where perpetuating one's faith seemed to be the exception rather than the norm.

20. How might doubt manifest itself in a family today? Consider especially subtle evidences of doubt such as prayerlessness.

Israel's Motivation to Love God

21. Read Deuteronomy 6:20–25. What question did Moses anticipate the Israelite children would ask in the future?

Moses wanted to equip the current generation to provide answers that perpetuated their faith in their children. Moses instructed the adults to answer by recounting their merciful redemption from Egypt. Israel's deliverance from Egypt was their fundamental motivation for loving God and living as consecrated to Him. Similarly, the redemption provided in Jesus Christ should motivate believers to love God and live for Him. When people ask why we believe and act the way we do, our answer should point them to Christ's redemption work on the cross.

MAKING IT PERSONAL

22. Have you ever felt as if God hated you? What were the circumstances?

23. Why are circumstances not a good gauge of God's love for you?

24. When you begin to doubt God's love for you, what steps will you take to counteract that doubt?

25. What might loving God with your whole being look like?

26. How might you grow your love for God this week?

I AM the Solid Rock

▶ Scripture Focus

Deut. 7—34

Theme

God as the Solid Rock is faithful to His people and His promises and worthy of our trust.

Memory Verses

"Because I will publish the name of the Lord: ascribe ye greatness unto our God. He is the Rock, his work is perfect: for all his ways are judgment: a God of truth and without iniquity, just and right is he" (Deuteronomy 32:3, 4).

GETTING STARTED

A swan song is someone's last performance or final accomplishment. The phrase *swan song* comes from an ancient legend about a swan. The legend says that the swan's only sound during its entire life is a song it sings right before it dies.

1. What would you like your swan song to be?

2. How have you been influenced by someone else's swan song?

The Bible passage for the final lesson in this course could be called Moses' swan song. In fact, he wrote his final words to Israel as a song. It puts their history and future as well as God's characteristics into focus.

Deuteronomy 7–31 repeats Israel's history and clarifies God's commandments. The new generations needed to hear God's law from Moses before he died and before they moved into the Promised Land. The overriding theme of the section is the need for Israel to love God for Who He is and What He has done for them. That theme reached its crescendo in Moses' song that ended his instructions to Israel (Deut. 32; 33). Moses sung about God as the Solid Rock and about Israel as the often unfaithful, rebellious nation.

Moses' Song

Moses' song begins with a call for creation to witness the judgment that is going to be revealed. The heavens and earth are fitting *witnesses* since Moses' message was of grand importance.

3. Read Deuteronomy 32:2. What effect did Moses want his teaching to have on the Israelites?

Rain and dew sustain life for plants. Moses wanted his words to be like rain that soaked into the ground and provided moisture for growth.

4. How might the Israelites soak in Moses' important words about God?

Moses began the heart of his song by praising God (32:3). To *publish the name of the Lord* means to point out God's qualities. His *name* then reflects His qualities. In anticipation of proclaiming God's name, Moses told the Israelites to *ascribe ye greatness unto our God* (32:3). To *ascribe greatness* means to *credit God with greatness*. Israel had many reasons to ascribe greatness to God. It should have come naturally for them as they reflected on their history. Later in the song Moses listed some of those reasons to ascribe greatness to God (32:7–14).

God deserved to be credited with greatness because He is the *Rock* (32:4). The name the *Rock* sums up how He had treated Israel since their beginning.

5. Read Deuteronomy 32:4. What are some qualities of God that remind you of a rock?

Moses added that God's *work is perfect* (32:4). There was never a moment in Israel's history in which God treated them less than perfectly. Yet there were many times Israel tried to make that case (Exod. 14:11, 12; 15:22–24; 16:2, 3; 17:1–3; Num. 11:4–6; 14:1–4). Israel believed any time they weren't completely happy with their circumstances that God had somehow wronged them. But in each instance they were the ones who were wrong.

Moses added the statement that *all His ways are judgment*, meaning *just* or *right* (Deut. 32:4). *Ways* is a reference to God's decisions. The word *all* left no room for arguing that God had ever made a choice that was tainted with *iniquity* or *injustice*. Conversely, He is a *God of truth*. He has no devious or impure motives driving His actions and decisions.

6. How should Israel have responded to God's record of perfect actions and motives?

Israel's Response to God's Person

Moses' words to describe God give the sense of unwavering straight-forwardness. His words to describe Israel are the opposite. Israel rejected God even though He treated them perfectly. Their rejection of Him was a corrupt response (32:5). God most notably called Israel's actions corrupt when they made and worshiped the gold calf (9:12). They gave to their idol the honor that was God's exclusively. That put a *spot* on them that was not the *spot* of God's children. In other words, they acted as if they didn't belong to God. Moses further described them as a *perverse and crooked generation*. *Perverse* conveys the idea of *warped* or *twisted*. The picture is of Israel wandering off the straight path God laid out for them.

Israel's warped and crooked condition prompted Moses to ask two questions. The first question asked them if this was the way they were going to repay (*requite*) the Lord (32:6). Such an action was *foolish* and *unwise*. A *fool* is someone who thinks he knows better than God and that his way is the right way. The Israelites were convinced that they were in the right and God was wrong.

The second question pointed out that God was Israel's Father in the sense that He had formed them as a nation and *established* them. Hence they were responsible to Him. To take a crooked path away from God made no sense. Moses wanted Israel to understand the folly of living according to their desires.

7. In what sense does every sin against God not make any sense?

God's Goodness to Israel

To make Israel's indictment even more serious, Moses went on to recount God's specific actions toward Israel. He introduced this section by calling on Israel to remember their past and to ask their elders to recount for them what God had done in their lifespans (32:7). This verse was for the current generation but also for the generations to come that would recite the song.

When God divided the nations He did so as the *Most High* (32:8) rather than as Yahweh, the name He used in His covenant relationship with Israel. God set Israel apart as His people and gave them Canaan to be their land. Israel was God's inheritance, the only nation with that special privilege (32:9).

The mention of a desert land in verse 10 is a reference to the early days of Israel's formation as God's chosen people. From that point in Israel's history, God protected them, directed them, and provided for them. To be the *apple* of God's *eye* means to be held as extremely dear by God.

8. Read Deuteronomy 32:11, 12. How does Moses point out that God deserved all the credit for leading and caring for Israel?

Moses looked ahead to the time when Israel would be in the Promised Land and listed some of the sumptuous foods they would enjoy there (32:13, 14). He would give them the best of the best as they lived off the land.

Israel's Response to God's Goodness

Moses, still looking to the future, knew what Israel's response would be. Rather than responding with loyalty to God's generous expressions of love, Israel would reject God, pursue idolatry, and forget the God Who formed them (32:15–18). *Jeshurun* (32:15) is a rare name for Israel. It is derived from a verb meaning *upright*. This passage's usage of *Jeshurun* creates a tragic irony; Israel is portrayed as anything but upright. *Jeshurun* is particularly tragic when set next to God's name, the *Rock*. Remember that is God's name that harkens back to His solid faithfulness throughout Israel's history.

9. Read Deuteronomy 32:17, 18. What descriptions of Israel's false gods make them sound so insignificant next to God, the Rock?

God's Response to Israel's Unfaithfulness

God *abhorred*, or *despised*, Israel for their idolatry (32:19). He said He would hide His face from them because of their lack of faith and their perverseness (32:20). When God shined His face on Israel they enjoyed His blessings. When God hid His face from Israel they experienced His chastening. God would work to turn Israel back to Himself by letting them see the inevitable results of their rebellion.

God is just in this judgment because Israel turned from Him to worship *that which is not God* and idols. God's *jealousy* motivated His judgment, meaning He loved Israel too much to let them wander from Him. God would execute His judgment by those *which are not a people* (32:21). This signifies that God would use the nations of the world to discipline His chosen people. Israel would witness terrifying bloodshed and destruction because of their infidelity to the Lord (32:22, 23). They would suffer hunger, attacks by beasts, and devastating attacks by invading armies. The armies would reach even into their homes, providing no safe place or retreat from the killing (32:24, 25). God would stay His hand only so that the invading armies would not credit themselves for the destruction instead of God (32:26, 27).

10. Read Deuteronomy 32:28, 29. Why would God reveal all this destruction to Israel right before they were to enter the Promised Land?

11. Read Deuteronomy 32:30. What is the point of the question in this verse?

Lest Israel's enemies think they are free from responsibility for their actions, Moses predicted their eventual destruction. Their *rock*, or *god*, is not like God, the *Rock* (32:31). God fights for His people and is mighty in power. God would take vengeance on Israel's enemies for their destructive cruelty (32:32–35).

The description of God's judgment is very severe (32:36). One could conclude that God will completely annihilate Israel in the latter days. But God will never abandon Israel.

12. Read Deuteronomy 32:36–38. What will Israel learn from God's judgment of their sinful idolatry?

God is the only true God. There are none beside Him at all. He controls the nations and the course of history. The arrows that pierced Israel would eventually pierce their enemies and no one could stop it (32:39–42). This reversal would be cause for the Gentiles to rejoice with God's people (32:43).

Moses' Application

The bleak picture of coming judgment was intended to motivate faithfulness and obedience in the Israelites' lives.

13. Read Deuteronomy 32:45–47. Why would it be worth the effort for Israel to strive to obey God?

Prophesies of judgment are to create anticipation in the reader by motivating the individual to avoid judgment.

14. Read Deuteronomy 32:51, 52. Why did God not allow Moses to enter the Promised Land?

The text's inclusion of God's instruction for Moses to die on Mount Nebo in this position seems strange at first (32:48–52). However, it serves as an emotionally charged reminder: no one is beyond receiving God's judgment. Even Moses, the friend of God (Exod. 33:11), could face judgment because of unbelief. He was an immediate example to the rest of the nation.

Moses' Blessing

Whereas Deuteronomy 32 focused on the judgment of Israel in the latter days, Deuteronomy 33 focuses on their eventual blessing. This final poem's form is very similar to Jacob's poetic blessing of Israel, the first major poem of the Pentateuch (Gen. 49).

Moses prefaced his blessings on the tribes by recalling when the Lord came down on Mount Sinai and gave Israel His law through Moses (Deut. 33:1–4). The Lord was motivated by His love for His people (33:3).

15. Read Deuteronomy 33:2, 3. What motivated God to leave Heaven to come to Mount Sinai and meet with the sinful Israelites?

16. What motivates God to have a relationship with us today? Are we so special that God can't help meeting with us?

The *king* in verse 5 could refer either to God or Moses. Most scholars see God as the King, though the context does allow for interpreting the king as Moses. While never an official king, Moses served as the authoritative, mediating leader of Israel.

The theme of *king* in Deuteronomy 33:5 perhaps links to the *king* promises found in Genesis 49:10 and Numbers 24:7–9. If Moses is the king in mind in Deuteronomy 33:5, then his identification as king in that passage should also be coupled with his role as priest. Moses met repeatedly with God and communicated God's law to the people. As a king, Moses would be similar to Melchizedek, the priest-king in Genesis 14:18–20.

Moses blessed the tribes of Israel by name in Deuteronomy 33:7–25. The structure of the blessing creates a structural link with Genesis 49. Both passages have an eschatological focus marked by a reference to the *latter days* in their introduction. And both passages project Israel's future.

In Genesis 49 the blessing of Judah is rather extended. By contrast Moses' blessing on Judah in Deuteronomy 33 encompasses only verse 7. The Deuteronomy passage assumes knowledge of the Genesis text.

The king theme in Deuteronomy 33 has already been injected with the introduction to the poem. So Moses' blessing of Judah emphasizes Judah's *military* role. That makes sense since the army of Judah was expected to lead the rest of the tribes into battle (Num. 2:9).

There is a cluster of words appearing in Deuteronomy 33 that are also clustered together in Genesis 15. Genesis 15 recounts God's covenant with Abraham. The common vocabulary of *help* (Deut. 33:7; Gen. 15:2), *covenant* (Deut. 33:9; Gen. 15:18), *righteousness* (Deut. 33:21; Gen. 15:6), *judge* (Deut. 33:22; Gen. 15:14), *possess* (Deut. 33:23; Gen. 15:4), *land* (Deut. 33:28; Gen. 15:7, 18), and *shield* (Deut. 33:29; Gen. 15:1) create a link between Moses' blessing of Israel and the covenantal promises given to Abraham. These groupings of words seem to point to an intentional connection between the two events. A definite Abrahamic covenant link is highlighted in Moses' view of the *latter days*.

There are several other links between Abraham's blessing and the rest of the Pentateuch. But the links referenced above are sufficient to confirm our understanding that the Pentateuch has a definite messianic orientation. Israel was to live each day by faith, trusting that God would fulfill His promises to provide the Messiah.

Moses concluded his blessing of Israel by returning his focus to the

nation as a whole (33:26–29). Like this poem's introduction, these verses
return to the theme of God's favor toward His chosen people. Ultimately
God's blessing of Israel is rooted in His character. He loves them, fights
for them, protects them, and blesses them because of Who He is.

The promises in Deuteronomy 33:28 and 29 should have given Israel
confidence as they approached the Promised Land. God would fight for
them, so victory was already assured. The Israelites' biggest struggle
would be within their hearts. Would they tread down the pagan high
places of worship, or would they embrace them instead? Ultimately,
Israel embraced pagan worship. So God sent them into captivity for their
disobedience.

But one day Israel will live in the land and fully realize God's promises to them such as those in Deuteronomy 33:28 and 29. Christ will rule
from His throne, and they will be happy in His presence.

Moses' Death

17. Read Deuteronomy 18:15. What did God promise in this verse?

Besides filling in the details of Moses' death, Deuteronomy 34 helps
us interpret the previous chapters and the Pentateuch as a whole. Deuteronomy 34:10 communicates there had not yet arisen a prophet like Moses
in Israel. This statement coupled with Deuteronomy 18:15 means Israel
needed to anticipate this future prophet.

We have already learned that Moses was presented as a priest-king; now
the role of prophet is added to that profile. The only person that can ultimately fulfill these three roles is the Messiah, Jesus Christ. So Deuteronomy 34:10
communicates that Israel should have been anticipating His arrival.

Christ did arrive eventually, but Israel rejected Him. He is coming
again, though. And we can look forward to His return.

MAKING IT PERSONAL

God is still the Solid Rock. He is as faithful as ever. He has never
veered onto a crooked or perverse path. We can trust Him completely and

never question His actions or His motives. We can look back at not only what He did for Israel but also at what He has done since, including His work in our own lives.

18. Which act of God on behalf of Israel bolsters your faith in Him?

19. What has God done in your life that gives you confidence in Him as the Solid Rock?

20. Review the major themes for each lesson. Which of the aspects of God's introduction to His people do you see reflected in Moses' song and blessing?

21. Which one do you need to consider in your relationship with God?